MY GRANDFATHER'S WAR

My Grandfather's War

A Young Man's Lessons
from the Greatest Generation

Jesse Cozean

LYONS PRESS
Guilford, Connecticut
An imprint of Globe Pequot Press

940.54
CO2   09/12

Lyons Press is an imprint of Globe Pequot Press.

Text design: Sheryl Kober
Project manager: Ellen Urban
Layout artist: Sue Murray

Library of Congress Cataloging-in-Publication Data is available on file.

ISBN 978-0-7627-7383-1

Printed in the United States of America

10 9 8 7 6 5 4 3 2 1

For my grandfathers, Robert P. Cozean and Patrick J. Day.
The only heroes I've ever had, or needed.

TABLE OF CONTENTS

CHAPTER 1

The Dam Bursts

THE STORY BEGINS IN 1920, 1944, 1986, OR 2008, DEPENDING ON your point of view. In 1920, my grandfather, Robert Cozean, was born in Missouri, less than a decade before the bottom fell out of the stock market and the onset of the Great Depression. In 1944, he was drafted to fight in World War II, went through basic training, and shipped off to fight Hitler. In 1986, I came crying into the world and Robert became Papa. But I think I'll start this story in 2008, simply because that's the only one of those dates I can remember.

Thanksgiving Day, 2008—I'm twenty-two, he's eighty-seven, and we're having a family dinner at my parents' house. I'm still living there, because after graduating from college with a degree in physics the thought of spending my life at a desk, slowly suffocating in a tie, is too terrifying to face. I was one of those members of my generation who didn't adapt quickly or well to the transition from the socially respected position of student to being unemployed with the toss of a graduation hat. So I was working nights as a waiter at an upscale barbecue place, doing some engineering and technical writing during the day, and waiting for my real life to begin.

At eighty-seven, Papa had only recently started to slow down. For the first time, he was spending the night in our guest room after Thanksgiving dinner, reluctantly obeying his doctor's suggestion to stop driving at night. Working with his hands for forty years as a successful carpenter had kept him strong. He was still driving (during the day, at least), going on exotic vacations, and living happily alone in the house he had built with his own hands sixty years earlier. The house was Papa's castle, built primarily of red brick and set off the street in an old neighborhood of Pasadena. A set of spiraling brick stairs led up to the front door. The whole house was infused with the smell of wood, drifting up—or so I imagined—from the cluttered woodshop in the basement. It came to be one of my favorite smells growing up. I had it on good authority that nothing inside the house had changed in the twenty years since my grandmother passed away.

His living room was filled with hideously uncomfortable antique sofas that no one would even consider sitting on, an out-of-tune piano that no one played, and an electronic organ. Papa didn't really know how to play the organ but loved messing around with it, playing a few different chords with his hands while stomping on the pedals with his feet, all with a huge smile on his face. Every time he played, the same melody would emerge, sometimes immediately and sometimes gradually sneaking into the seemingly random set of chords, until I would start humming along. "Oh when the saints, go marching in, oh when the saints go mar-ching in . . ."

His family inherited both his love of music and his reluctance to practice very hard. My dad is very good on the flute, can pick out a few chords on the piano, and recently decided to be terrible at the hammer dulcimer. In his defense, it looks like an incredibly hard instrument to play. It's basically a harp turned on its side, or the innards of a piano pulled out and set on display. The strings are supposed to be expertly struck with tiny mallets. My father has no fine motor control—his signature is so bad, he often has to sign a form, somehow presented without a trace of irony, that asserts that his signature is, in fact, a signature—so I'm not sure why he thought the dulcimer would be a good idea. Of course, if I understood his motivation, I would also understand why I just bought a harmonica. I also play the guitar reasonably well, at least better than the piano, which I play even worse than my dad. I blame Papa for all the dissonant noise reverberating around the house.

My earliest memories of my grandfather are indelibly inter-twined with the rhymes of Dr. Seuss, which may explain why the few wispy gray hairs he had left always reminded me of the Lorax. Every Wednesday, Papa and my mother's parents would drive down from Pasadena to pick me up and take me out to lunch. I would sit on the curb outside of the elementary school office with my nose in a colorful Dr. Seuss book until they arrived. The musty aroma of his house would travel with Papa, and I could always smell it on him when I wrapped him in a tight hug. We would go out to Sizzler, the only place I could have my favorite childhood meal—chicken tenders dipped in chocolate mousse.

Papa's wife passed away when I was four years old. They had the kind of marriage that is always presented as idyllic in the old black-and-white movies, meeting at the church youth group and marrying young, before he went off to war. When he came home Papa was the breadwinner, going off to work honorably with his hands and provide for his family while she stayed home to cook, clean, and raise the kids. Their two children, Keith and my father

3

Kim, were born nine years apart, begging the question which one (or both?) was the "accident" child. The boys were never that close; by the time my father developed a personality, Keith was already out of the house. My dad might have been the only kid to ever have his older brother coach his Little League team.

Finding himself alone after decades of married life, Papa quickly had to learn how to do all the things his wife had always handled around the house. Gradually he learned how to cook, at least well enough to stave off starvation. When in doubt, he would toss a potato in the microwave to bake for a few minutes. For my visits, he would make a special meal: frozen chicken tenders. Woefully unaware of how much a little boy needed to eat, he would always ask me if I wanted one or two of the bite-sized pieces. Starting that low in the negotiations, I was lucky to end up with three. Looking back, I wonder if he had just bought one big Costco bag when I was about five and used it to feed me for the next decade. One thing Papa always did have was a huge selection of jam, butter, and ketchup packets—a collection eerily similar to those found in the restaurants he frequented.

Learning to cook was tough for Papa, but figuring out his finances was even more difficult. Like many of his generation, he just brought home his paychecks and handed them to his wife. After her death, for the first time in nearly forty years, he had to pay his own bills and keep track of the money. Just a few days after my grandmother passed away, my mother had to take off work and drive up to Pasadena to teach Papa how to write a check in order to pay the hospital bill. To make things even more complicated, my grandparents had learned the lessons of the Great Depression well. No single bank was going to fail and take their life savings with it, even if the government was supposed to be insuring the accounts. Their money was squirrelled away in half a dozen different banks, and it was not until the next January, when the banks sent out their annual statements, that Papa knew he had located all of it. Tellingly, not a penny they saved ever entered the stock market.

As the years passed, Papa began dating again, with considerable success. Evidently if you are a single man over seventy-five, you don't have much trouble finding a canasta partner, especially if your mode of transport is a car and not a walker. I remember several of his girlfriends over the years, but the one that he eventually settled on was a sweet little lady named Pat. They met while working together in their church's soup kitchen, serving food to the homeless once a month. He would bring her to our holiday dinners, where he was always decked out in a festive red flannel vest. The two of them were always travelling together, heading off on a cruise to Alaska, visiting Seattle, or driving down to Vegas to catch a show. When they had been dating about five years, Pat's sister-in-law, Mary, lost her husband to cancer. Mary gradually joined their travelling group, becoming a constant third wheel who provided some much-needed vitality and "youth" to their entourage, as she was about ten years younger. We referred to them as a single entity requiring three seats at holiday dinners; "Papa and the Girls" were nearly inseparable.

When the three of them took a road trip together, they travelled in style. Well after he turned eighty, Papa went down to a dealership for a new car. He must have asked for the one you would be most surprised to see an old person in, because he came back with a lustrous Chrysler 300. It sported a huge grill splashed across the front and an engine that roared instead of purred; he completed the look by outfitting it with gleaming chrome rims.

I'm sure the car and its gray-haired occupants caused a few passing drivers to do a double take on the road to Vegas—if anyone managed to pass him.

My family has always been close-knit, at least in the sense that we always eat together on holidays, make sure we get together every few months, and never argue or fight. But truthfully, we're a pretty emotionally closed-off bunch. There are only three acceptable conversational topics for men in my family: the best driving route from Point A to Point B, the success or failure of the local sports teams, and whatever stupid thing Congress has done lately (providing, of course, it doesn't lead to a well-rounded discussion of the issue at hand). Papa and my dad were so good at discussing driving routes they often didn't need to move on to the other potential topics. In order to participate without a road map in my hands, I would wait until the matter was nearly settled, stroke my chin and thoughtfully raise a question that brought everything into doubt once again. "Ah, but what if it's raining?" Embracing the challenge, they would start in again, plotting new routes and easily killing the twenty minutes before the food was finished and we could turn our attention to eating. We had our family patterns and were quite comfortable in them, which made it even more shocking when, just after his eightieth birthday, Papa began bringing up his time as a prisoner of war in Germany.

Of course, I had always known that he had served in World War II and been captured, just like I had always known the stories about my grandmother and the building of their house. It's that peculiar type of family memory, where someone has obviously told you but you were too young to remember actually hearing it, so it seems like knowledge that was instilled at birth. Papa never brought it up, and my parents said they hadn't heard him mention it once in the previous fifty years. But suddenly, he was talking. It was like a dam inside him had finally burst, and he needed to tell his story. It came up in every conversation with him, without segue or warning. I don't think anyone in my family was very comfortable hearing him start to open up about his time in the German POW camp. It's not a topic that lends itself to holiday cheer or easily leads to other conversations, and our response after hearing a particularly detailed story was usually an awkward silence, followed by an abrupt subject change: "So, those Dodgers—think they're going to win the division this year?"

When Papa began talking about World War II, he sought out others who had shared his experiences. The bond between the survivors was so strong it overcame half a century of neglect after they returned home. Papa began attending conventions for ex-POWs, meeting old friends from his unit or camps, and hearing the accounts of men who had been imprisoned in other camps in Germany. The men would share their experiences at an open microphone, letting go of the traumatic memories they had bottled up inside. Many, like Papa, had never spoken of their time as prisoners, even with their closest friends or family. When the former POWs got together, there was never any mention of rank. There is only one rank for a POW—they were all survivors, whether they had worn the stars of a general or the single chevron of a private.

— ~ —

Trapped. I had foolishly wandered into the kitchen for a late-night, post-Thanksgiving snack and failed to escape before Papa noticed me. He was spending the night to avoid driving home in the dark. When he called me over I knew I was in for another lecture about his time as a prisoner of war, probably one that I had heard several times before. Standing there, helpless, my two scoops of ice cream beginning to soften in the bowl, I felt like a prisoner myself as he fired the opening salvo in his plaid nightshirt. "Do you know how many POWs there were in World War II?"

The question was an ambush, like the one his company had fallen into during the Battle of the Bulge. Failing to know would provoke a well-meaning discourse on the large number of prisoners that were captured and the general ignorance of my generation. A correct answer—the number is around 130,000, as I had heard several times before—would be seen as an expression of renewed interest and an encouragement to continue. Fiercely aware that the ambient temperature of the house would not support ice cream in a solid form, I hoped to tread the thin line between both answers and escape with both his feelings and my mint chocolate treat intact.

Though it might sound cold or heartless, my lack of interest was more a result of his poor timing and storytelling skills than anything else. I always listened politely, but the tales tended to spill out indiscriminately. Often the same story was favored several days in a row, always recounted at times that made it difficult to pay full attention. We would be opening presents on Christmas or taking our first bite of birthday cake and he would suddenly, almost compulsively, start talking about the prison camp. My parents thought it was because he had kept the memories bottled up for so long, either because that was standard for men of his generation or because his wife didn't like hearing about it. Now, finally, he was able to satisfy his need to tell his family about what he had been through. Of course, not only his family was subject to Papa's stories; waitresses, bank tellers, telemarketers—no one was safe. Frequently I would be standing next to him when he started in, embarrassed and trying to apologize with my body language to whomever he had cornered.

He seemed most comfortable talking about his time in World War II with me, though I'm not sure why. Perhaps because he and my father hadn't discussed it when my dad was growing up, that habit of silence was hard to break. My dad did appear to be more uncomfortable with the choice of topic than anyone else in the family. Maybe Papa chose his audience by the process of elimination—my sister was ruled out because she was a girl, my uncle Keith and his kids were too far away and didn't see Papa very often, and my mother was usually in the kitchen making the meals, a room we avoided to prevent being assigned a job chopping vegetables or stirring a sauce. My guess is that it was because, at twenty-two, I was about the same age he was when he was drafted and sent to the front lines, and that sparked his memory. Whatever the reason, I seemed to bear the brunt of his storytelling. And on that Thanksgiving night, I was more concerned about finishing my snack and getting some sleep than listening to my grandfather.

But as we talked, the former prisoner and the current one, I had something that I think can only be described as an epiphany, as clichéd as it sounds. In the tradition of my family I'm not much of a crier, but I found myself holding back tears as I listened to the stories that I had heard many times before. Maybe it was because my grandfather was able to tell me a full story, without being rushed or distracted, or maybe I was finally just ready to listen. The rust was somehow scraped away, and the realization of what my kindly grandfather had endured—this man who had taken me to innumerable Sizzler buffets, faithfully watched my basketball games when my legs were so short I had to lift a leg to dribble between them, taught me how to shoot pool in his musty basement—finally began to sink in.

I have always wanted to be a writer. A love of language and a passionate hatred of ties, cubicles, time clocks, and bosses leaves few other options. But that night was the first time I felt a calling to write, to find and share the infinitely varied, mundane and miraculous, hilarious and heartbreaking stories of other people, the ones we brush aside, gloss over, or never really have a chance to hear, the stories that slip past before we even realize what we are missing.

I listened—really listened—to Papa for over an hour that night. After he finally tired and fell asleep, I went upstairs to my room and wrote down as much as I could remember of the stories he had told. My final entry in that notebook reads: "There is so much wonder in this world of ours. Perhaps the greatest wonder is that we can't, or won't, see it." I had ignored it for years in my grandfather. Maybe that was why he was trying so hard to get his story told; it seemed like the world, and his family, had missed it.

CHAPTER 2

Going to War

I am in the infantry and I guess I will stay there. You can't transfer out, so they say. I wish I was back in California. That train ride was awful . . . I would give anything in the world to get out of this jail.
—ROBERT COZEAN, LETTER FROM TRAINING CAMP IN CAMP FANNIN, TEXAS, 1944

We sure do appreciate getting the picture. I cannot say that I like it. Of course we wanted it, but I like you better without the uniform. Love, Mom and Dad
—BRYAN COZEAN, LETTER TO HIS SON ROBERT, 1944

MOST HISTORIANS CONSIDER THE BEGINNING OF WORLD WAR II to be September 1, 1939, when Germany launched a surprise, but hardly unexpected, invasion of Poland. It had become apparent, ever since Hitler and the Nazis came to power in 1933, that Germany wanted to expand and avenge their loss in World War I. Using the presence of German-speaking Poles as an excuse, Hitler planned to "liberate" Poland and began massing troops along the border.

Poland, clearly outnumbered in manpower and outclassed in equipment, was dependent on her allies in the event of an attack. Britain and France planned to use Poland as a buffer, anticipating it would take Germany two to three months to conquer the country—time they would use to bring troops in and mount a counterattack. In a treaty signed fewer than eighteen months before the outbreak of war, they promised to do exactly that.

Prior to the attack, Hitler was conducting last-minute negotiations with Stalin and the Soviet Union. Before invading Poland he had to be convinced that the powerful Red Army would not intervene on the side of the Poles. Stalin and Hitler, despite sharing places on the short list of most brutal dictators in the world, were ideological enemies. So it was a stunning negotiating coup when Hitler signed a treaty with the Russians only a week before the invasion. Not only did Stalin agree not to interfere but, in return for a piece of Poland and the promise of more territory in Eastern Europe, he promised to come to the aid of Germany if the UK or France attacked over Poland. By the time the German armies poured over the border in three separate attacks, Hitler was certain that Great Britain and France would not risk intervening against the combined military power of Germany and the USSR. Poland was on its own.

The German tanks and infantry smashed through the overmatched Polish Army on the border, intent on encircling and destroying the Polish divisions. Before the invasion, Hitler told his generals:

Our strength is our speed and our brutality. Genghis Khan chased millions of women and children to death, consciously and with a happy heart. History sees him only as a great founder of states. It is of no concern, what the weak Western European civilization is saying about me. I issued the command—and I will have everybody executed, who will only utter a single word of criticism—that it is not the aim of the war to reach particular lines, but to physically annihilate the enemy.

It only took nine days for German troops to reach Warsaw, the capital of Poland. The Polish Army continued a fighting retreat, bleeding to buy time for France and England to come to their aid. All hope was lost when eight hundred thousand soldiers of the Red Army poured across the Polish border with the USSR. Against the combined might of Germany and the Soviet Union, Poland didn't stand a chance. Orders came not to oppose the advance of the Russians, and the remnants of the Polish Army retreated into the neutral country of Romania or fled into France. The entire conquest was complete only thirty-six days after the first German tanks surged across the border.

While the German tanks were blasting through the Polish defenses and starting the war in Europe, Papa was enrolled at Frank Wiggins Trade School learning to be a carpenter. He had always loved wood, and growing up in the Great Depression, he was already well versed in working with his hands. At the time, college was a luxury that few could afford. The battles an ocean away didn't concern Papa—he was enjoying school and travelling across California on the weekends and summer breaks. He and some friends climbed Mount Whitney back when it was the highest peak in the country (Alaska didn't become a state until 1959) and took hiking trips in Yosemite. In 1939 it was still possible to ignore the war looming on the horizon. Finding work was easier as America was being pulled out of the Depression by military spending, and the future was bright for my grandfather.

Though France and Great Britain declared war on Germany two days after the invasion of Poland, the wider war didn't break out until May of 1940, eight months later. In the intervening time the Soviet Union moved troops into the Baltic States, and Germany invaded Denmark and Norway. Denmark surrendered immediately, and Norway, fighting with Allied support, lasted only two months against a small portion of the German Army. The French, knowing they would be next, prepared for war by heavily reinforcing the border with Germany.

On May 10, 1940, Germany invaded France, along with Belgium, the Netherlands, and Luxembourg. On the same day in Great Britain, Prime Minister Neville Chamberlain resigned and was replaced by Winston Churchill. The Germans' armored divisions punched massive holes in the defenses of the Netherlands and Belgium, and both countries were overrun within weeks. The French, confident in their line of concrete fortifications, antitank weapons, and machine gun nests placed along the border with Germany, believed they could throw back any German attack. Instead of a frontal assault on the French lines, the Germans moved through the thick woods of the Ardennes, which the French mistakenly believed would be impassable for the armored columns. By skirting the main defenses, the Germans were able to avoid the initial line of defense and proceeded to flank and encircle the French troops. The defenders were pinned back, trapped against their own fortifications. The heavy forests of the Ardennes would prove to be the backdrop for another massive battle in a few short years and serve as the setting for my grandfather's capture.

Shockingly, by the end of the month France was all but defeated. The Allies were completely unprepared for a modern war. In World War I, men would spend months battling over a few yards of trenches and barbed wire. Now, only a little more than two decades later, Hitler and the Third Reich had taken less than a month to conquer all of France, Belgium, the Netherlands, and tiny Luxembourg. British and French troops were driven to the edge of Europe and pinned back against the sea. The core of the Royal Army was about to be destroyed when a flotilla of more than 850 ships, almost entirely civilian volunteers, arrived to rescue the trapped soldiers. The fishing boats, private yachts, and merchant marine ships evacuated 338,226 soldiers from the beaches of Dunkirk over the course of nine days. Soldiers would wade out into the ocean as far as they could, lining up to be saved in the shoulder-deep water. The smaller civilian vessels were invaluable, as they were able to move into the shallow water and ferry the men to larger ships waiting farther off shore. In the air above the evacuation, the Royal Air Force (RAF) engaged in a desperate attempt to cover the evacuation from the fire of German Luftwaffe planes. The rescuing boats came under relentless attack from the air, and more than two hundred were sunk during the evacuation. Left behind on the beaches were 2,472 guns, sixty-five thousand vehicles, and seventy-five thousand tons of ammunition. Two French divisions remained behind as a rearguard, fighting to protect the evacuation, and were soon captured.

Hitler had missed the opportunity to crush the core of the Royal Army at Dunkirk. Without those troops, Great Britain would have been overwhelmingly outnumbered, and the Axis powers could have invaded the island, effectively ending the war before the United States decided to join in. In retrospect, the bravery of the fishing vessels, yachts, and merchant ships was one of the most important moments of World War II.

Those soldiers captured at Dunkirk were taken on foot back into Germany, a march that took twenty days to complete. By June 1940, only ten months after the first shots of World War II were fired, Great Britain stood alone against Germany, the Soviet Union, and their allies. In a famous speech after the fall of France, Winston Churchill addressed his nation with words that still send a shiver up the spine, even seventy years later:

> *Hitler knows that he will have to break us in this Island or lose the war. If we can stand up to him, all Europe may be free and the life of the world may move forward into broad, sunlit uplands. But if we fail, then the whole world, including the United States, including all that we have known and cared for, will sink into the abyss of a new Dark Age made more sinister, and perhaps more protracted, by the lights of perverted science.*
>
> *Let us therefore brace ourselves to our duties, and so bear ourselves that if the British Empire and its Commonwealth last for a thousand years, men will still say, "This was their finest hour."*

Even as Hitler conquered all of continental Europe, the United States remained stubbornly neutral, afraid of being drawn into another European war. Despite the protests of President Franklin D. Roosevelt, the American Congress passed four separate Neutrality Acts from 1936 to 1939. These acts prohibited America from selling arms or war materials to any country involved

in the conflict, as well as from loaning money to any combat-
ant. In an effort to circumvent these laws, President Roosevelt
pushed for and passed an exception for cash-and-carry weapons purchases. This provision allowed a country to buy guns and
ammunition from the United States, as long as they paid cash
and transported the weapons themselves. Congress believed that
this would allow the United States to make a quick buck without
becoming involved in the conflict. Roosevelt hoped that when
war broke out, British naval superiority would allow the Allies to
take advantage of the loophole.

The roots of America's strong aversion to entering the conflict can be traced back to the Great War and the Great Depression. America had been drawn into the last European war and
had won—according to the history books, at least—at great
cost in currency and lives. At the height of the war, the United
States was sending ten thousand men a day to fight and die in
Europe. All told, more than sixty-eight million men fought in
the trenches of World War I, for the first time facing machine
guns, mustard gas, airplanes, and tanks in combat. Nearly ten million men were left dead on the field of battle, and twenty million
more were wounded. When the war ended with the Treaty of
Versailles in 1918, the United States, Great Britain, France, and
the other Allies stood victorious. The Austro-Hungarian, German,
and Ottoman Empires were defeated and disintegrated, reshaping
the European landscape. The Russian Empire also collapsed and
was replaced by the communist Soviet Union. However, the outcome of the war had no direct benefit for the American people. The
reshaping of the European borders was purely academic to people
who had lost friends and family members in the war. And less than
two decades after the conclusion of "The War to End All Wars,"

Europe was once again arming for a conflict that would engulf the entire continent. The American people were tired of being drawn into Europe's wars. The last had proved there was no benefit to fighting in foreign conflicts, and there were more than enough problems on this side of the Atlantic.

The economic hardships caused by the Great Depression were much more real to the average American than geopolitical events an ocean away. When the stock market crashed on Black Tuesday, 1929, it sent the economy into an unprecedented free fall. By 1933, the stock market had lost 90 percent of its value. Nearly half of the country's banks had closed, costing many families their life savings. Before the market crashed, the unemployment rate in America was three percent—three years later, one in three Americans was without a job, and wages were slashed for nearly everyone. Shantytowns sprang up across the country, filled with the newly homeless. They were mockingly known as Hoovervilles, after the sitting president. The U.S. government categorized 60 percent of the country as below the poverty line and, for the first time since Columbus landed, more people were leaving the United States than entering.

Papa was nine years old when the Great Depression hit. His family lived in Missouri, where his mother ran the post office and his father sold insurance. They scraped by, mostly on her salary, as people who could still afford insurance—or who had anything left to insure—were rare. The most enduring memory my grandfather shared of his childhood was playing in the mine tailings. Tailings are the piles of rock and sludge left over once all the valuable ore is taken out. Today they are the biggest environmental hazard of mining, containing dangerous heavy metals and toxic chemicals like cyanide. Eighty years ago, they were a playground where

Papa and other children would sit on pieces of scrap metal and skid down the rock piles.

Though he had a large extended family in the area, Papa was an only child. Children of that era were often named after famous historical figures. There is a George Washington Cozean in our family's genealogy. Papa's father evidently didn't rate quite so highly—he was christened William Jennings Bryan Cozean, after the orator and politican who lost presidential elections in 1896, 1900, and 1908. Today William Jennings Bryan is best remembered for his work as the prosecutor in the Scopes Monkey Trial, where he persuaded the court to find a schoolteacher guilty for teaching evolution in the classroom. Of course, Papa's father was already a middle-aged man with a son of his own before the conclusion of the trial. It's always wise to wait until a politician is safely dead before you name your son after him. And perhaps that's why Papa's father always went by Bryan.

With the country reeling from the Great Depression, Roosevelt won a landslide victory on promises of a New Deal for the country. As president he began attempts to put America back to work, and was at least successful in mitigating the symptoms of the economic meltdown. With war on the horizon in 1940, he was elected to an unprecedented third term.

With the recent example of World War I and the hardship of the Great Depression, it is easy to understand why many Americans wanted to remain aloof from the turmoil in Europe. However, it would not be long until Roosevelt's famous quote, "when peace has been broken anywhere, the peace of all countries everywhere is in danger," became prophetic. After the fall of France in 1940, Germany began aggressively attacking British shipping. The United States agreed to create a security zone, halfway across the Atlantic, where they would protect international trading. This put the U.S. Navy into confrontations with German U-boats and created a clandestine naval war in the Atlantic. The United States also agreed to trade Britain fifty naval destroyers for the rights to military bases in British territories. America was finding it more and more difficult to remain neutral.

— —

For exactly a year, from June 22, 1940, to June 22, 1941, the tiny island of Great Britain bore the brunt of the Axis attacks alone. A massive German bombing campaign struck the island nightly, seeking to destroy British shipping and harbor facilities, RAF airfields, and the country's infrastructure. If the Luftwaffe gained air superiority, the Axis powers could launch an invasion of their last remaining rival. As they continued to meet strong opposition from the RAF, the Luftwaffe began terror bombings of British cities. At one point, civilians in London were bombed for fifty-seven consecutive days. Parents sent their children out of the city, to relatives or friends or even strangers in the country, and fled themselves if they were able. During this time, the British Army also fought Germany and her allies in Africa, the Middle East, and Greece, attempting to halt the expansion of fascism.

The first half of 1941 was a dark time for those who opposed Hitler. The Third Reich controlled Germany, Austria, Poland, Czechoslovakia, Denmark, Norway, Greece, the Netherlands, Belgium, Luxembourg, and France. It wasn't surprising that they easily defeated Poland, although they had been able to do so in less than half the time the Allies believed possible. But the absolute annihilation of France's army—one of the largest and most powerful in Europe—was truly shocking, especially considering it had been achieved in less than a month. Italy was part of the Axis powers, and Spain's fascist dictator, General Franco, also supported Germany. The USSR, which had entered an agreement with Hitler, was in possession of parts of Poland and the Baltic States. Hungary, Bulgaria, Slovakia, and Romania had formally joined the Axis powers. Sweden was technically neutral, but had allowed German troops to cross its country in order to invade Norway. Sweden also sold iron, vital to the war effort, to the fascist countries. In Africa, British forces had been driven out of Libya and were barely holding onto Egypt. In the Pacific, Japan had successfully invaded China, French Indochina, Singapore, Hong Kong, the Dutch East Indies, and Malaya. The United States was clinging to neutrality and would not enter the war for another six months. Great Britain was truly alone.

As I read more about the war, I began to imagine what it must have been like for those about to be drafted and sent to the front lines. The outcome of World War II is so imprinted in our minds—good guys win, bad guys lose—it is hard to remember that when young men like Papa were preparing for the army, victory was anything but assured. All of continental Europe was controlled by Germany or her allies within a year—a goal that had eluded Napoleon, Charlemagne, and even the Roman Empire. Had Hitler annihilated the remains of the British Army at the beaches of Dunkirk, the United States could have easily been faced with all of Europe united under the swastika. Looking at history without the benefit of hindsight reveals how close to the precipice the world came.

While Europe was burning, the Empire of Japan was also seeking to expand. The policy of aggressive Japanese imperialism began nearly fifty years earlier. China, divided by competing warlords, was easy prey for Japan's well-trained army. The military leaders of Japan realized how vulnerable their country was, because it was severely lacking in important war materials like iron and oil. To become a true world power, they would need the resources that China possessed. The Empire of Japan launched repeated attacks on her larger neighbor, seizing the islands of Taiwan and Mongolia, and the natural resources that were vital to Japan's ambitions.

In a situation eerily similar to that in Germany, Japan was convinced of their racial superiority and imperial destiny. The entire country had militarized, much as Nazi Germany had, beginning with the youth. Schools became indoctrination centers, where children were taught the discipline they would need in the military and the righteousness of Japanese expansion. Just as the Hitler Youth served as a breeding ground for the SS and Gestapo in Europe, the schools of Japan began the physical and mental training that created the strongest military in the region.

Finally, in July of 1937, after years of smaller skirmishes, Japan launched a full invasion of China. Within three months, Japanese forces captured Shanghai and continued advancing, capturing the capital city of Nanking by December. The victory was followed by a six-week reign of terror known to history as the Rape of Nanking.

After two days of fighting, the Chinese forces defending their capital fled. The Japanese attackers moved in, easily securing the city. After the Imperial Army claimed the city walls and exterminated the remaining defenders, they turned their attention to the civilians of the city. The soldiers broke down doors and dragged the women, including children and the elderly, out of their homes and raped them repeatedly, before killing them. The International Military Tribunal for the Far East estimates that at least twenty thousand women were treated this way. The atrocities extended to men as well. The captured Chinese prisoners, an estimated fifty-seven thousand of them, were taken out into the fields, handcuffed together, and mowed down with machine gun fire. Another thirteen hundred surrendered soldiers and civilians were taken out to the city gate, doused with gasoline, and set on fire. Men, women and children were buried alive by the occupying troops—all justified by the belief in Japan's racial superiority.

During this period, a group of twenty-two European and American businessmen and missionaries stayed within the city, working to help the Chinese people. They were headed by an unlikely leader, John Rabe, a German businessman and member of the Nazi Party. With the Japanese army closing in, the group created the Nanking Safety Zone, an area that the Imperial Army promised to leave alone if Chinese soldiers did not seek refuge there. Armed only with his Nazi Party badge, Rabe worked tirelessly to protect as many innocents as he could. He sheltered hundreds of refugees on his personal property, and fed thousands more. His constant appeals to Japanese leaders on behalf of the Chinese citizens were at least heard, because Japan was concerned about his ability, as a member of the Nazi Party, to damage the alliance between Germany and Japan.

In a letter to the occupying authorities, four days after the fall of the city, Rabe wrote:

In other words, on the 13th when your troops entered the city, we had nearly all the civilian population gathered in a Zone

*in which there had been very little destruction by stray shells
and no looting by Chinese soldiers . . . our Chinese population
were totally surprised by the reign of robbery, raping and killing initiated by your soldiers on the 14th. All we are asking
in our protest is that you restore order among your troops and
get the normal city life going as soon as possible.*

It is estimated that Rabe and his efforts saved more than two
hundred thousand lives during the Rape of Nanking, but the
devastation of that city remains one of the greatest atrocities of
World War II.

While Japanese soldiers were destroying Nanking, Papa was
facing a common terror for any kid: entering a new high school.
When he was sixteen, his family moved from Missouri to California, opening a grocery store when they arrived in Los Angeles.
He entered Lincoln High School as a junior. Papa struggled with a
slight stammer and a fear of public speaking, making the transition
more difficult. He fit in by playing sports, beginning the tradition
of highly mediocre basketball playing that I proudly carried on.
Papa was also quite the ladies' man, judging from the comments
left in his yearbook—a trait that was evidently sloshed out of the
gene pool before I came around. Donning his cap and gown in
1938, Papa was graduating at the worst possible time.

After the invasion of China, the Imperial Army turned its
attention toward land in the Soviet Union. However, two important military defeats in Soviet territory convinced Japan's military
leadership and the emperor to seek easier gains elsewhere—in the
Pacific. Japan attacked and seized French Indochina (modern-
day Vietnam, Laos, and Cambodia), and in response the United
States cut off oil exports to Japan. The United States supplied

80 percent of Japan's oil, so Japan would have to either seize oil supplies by force or abandon their military expansion. With the European countries preparing for the inevitable attack from Germany, Japan knew that the United States represented the sole threat to their ambitions in the Pacific.

In September of 1940, Japan signed the Tripartite Pact with Germany and Italy, formalizing the Axis Powers. If anyone went to war with one of the countries, they went to war with all three.

On December 7, 1941, the United States was jolted out of neutrality by Japanese bombs screaming down on the fleet at Pearl Harbor. More than 350 Japanese planes struck the naval base, with the goal of preventing the United States from challenging Japan's expansion in the Pacific. The Japanese aircraft launched from a fleet of six aircraft carriers—three more than the entire U.S. Navy possessed at the time. Torpedo planes, bombers, and fighters plunged out of the sky above the ships at harbor and the planes and airfields on the island.

The attack was a complete surprise and a military disaster for the United States. Many of the ships in the harbor had only skeleton crews aboard, and planes were parked on runways wingtip to wingtip, perfect targets for Japanese strafing. The attack destroyed or heavily damaged all eight battleships at the base and almost all of the four hundred aircraft stationed there. The cost in lives totaled more than two thousand servicemen and fifty civilians.

While the attack succeeded in severely damaging the naval power of the United States, it also enraged and united a nation. Gone was America's neutrality. Instead of dissuading the country from entering the war, as Japan had hoped, the surprise raid galvanized public support for the war effort. The very next day, in a speech requesting that Congress declare war on Japan, President

Roosevelt began with the now well-known phrase, "Yesterday, December 7, 1941—a date which will live in infamy—the United States of America was suddenly and deliberately attacked by naval and air forces of the Empire of Japan." He continued:

Japan has, therefore, undertaken a surprise offensive extending throughout the Pacific area. The facts of yesterday and today speak for themselves. The people of the United States have already formed their opinions and well understand the implications to the very life and safety of our nation.

As commander in chief of the Army and Navy, I have directed that all measures be taken for our defense. But always will our whole nation remember the character of the onslaught against us.

No matter how long it may take us to overcome this premeditated invasion, the American people in their righteous might will win through to absolute victory.

I believe that I interpret the will of the Congress and of the people when I assert that we will not only defend ourselves to the uttermost, but will make it very certain that this form of treachery shall never again endanger us.

Hostilities exist. There is no blinking at the fact that our people, our territory, and our interests are in grave danger.

With confidence in our armed forces, with the unbounding determination of our people, we will gain the inevitable triumph, so help us God.

I ask that the Congress declare that since the unprovoked and dastardly attack by Japan on Sunday, December 7, 1941, a state of war has existed between the United States and the Japanese empire.

Within the hour Congress voted to declare war on Japan and the United States entered World War II.

— —

When the declaration of war came, Papa had graduated from trade school and found work in a carpentry shop. With the threat of war looming, the government had instituted the first peacetime draft in history several months before the attack on Pearl Harbor. Papa was deferred from the draft for a year because the shop where he worked was producing airplane seats, toolboxes, and extra gas containers for the war effort. It was a good thing he was, for both him and me—the delay gave him time to put a ring on the finger of Kathleen "Kitty" Anderson, the woman who would become my grandmother.

They had met at the church youth group, where Kitty, like many other girls, had been enchanted by my grandfather's bright blue eyes and charming ways. This time the feeling was mutual, and the near-certainty that Papa would have to fight in Europe or the Pacific accelerated their relationship. They were married on February 18, 1942, about two months after America joined the war.

After the wedding, the newlyweds moved in together and Kitty found a job as a secretary at an engineering firm. They had big plans for the future; Papa wanted to build a new house that they could fill with a family, but it was only a matter a time before he was called to serve. The government was drafting an astounding two hundred thousand men a month, inducting more than ten million men into service over the course of the war.

After two years of wedded bliss, Papa's number was finally called. He was ordered to report to Camp Fannin in Texas, where he spent seven weeks in basic training, learning everything the U.S. Army decreed was essential for a soldier to know—how to march, dig a foxhole, shoot a rifle, and follow orders. Many wives followed their husbands to basic training, renting an apartment near the base. Papa and Kitty agreed it would be foolish to spend the money and uproot Kitty from her friends, family, and a solid job for just a few extra weeks together.

Kitty meticulously saved every letter that Papa wrote, just as he filed all her letters that reached him in a box that would survive the war and was safely interned in the back of a closet in their home, untouched for nearly sixty years when I opened it. That box was a treasure to me as I tried to understand what Papa had gone through. In reading his scrawled handwriting, my grandfather's life began to snap into focus. He was twenty-three, in love and homesick, far away from not only his wife, but his parents and friends as well. The newspapers were making it clear that the Allies were massing men and equipment for the invasion of German-conquered Europe, and he knew that in just a few short months he would complete training and be shipped to the front lines. No wonder his thoughts lingered on what he would be leaving behind.

As soon as he was ordered out to basic training he began writing to his young wife, the letters pouring in nearly every day. Full of the optimism that characterized his life, they show both the pain of separation and hope for the future.

March 20, 1944
Dearest Kitty,
Today I got the bad news. I am shipping out, where to I don't know yet. I will write you a letter as soon as I can and tell

you where I am going. I feel awful funny now that I know I am shipping out—something just hit me funny. The thought of being far away from you sends chills up my back . . . I guess it had to come sooner or later. But we have a lot to be thankful for that I stayed here this long. I just pray that I am not shipped too far away so I can go home once in a while. Just think of the good times we have together and then you will know I am always thinking about you. I love you, oh so much. It is better to be shipped out the first weeks instead of the last week so don't worry too much about it. I might not go far if my luck holds!
Lots of love,
Bob

Like many of the men drafted away from families and home, Papa didn't have a lot of good things to say about training camp.

March 27, 1944
Dear Kitty,
We arrived Friday about 3 o'clock at Camp Fannin, Texas. So far it is the bunk. Red clay soil hard and dusty.
I am in the infantry and I guess I will stay there. You can't transfer out, so they say. I wish I was back in California. That train ride was awful . . . I sure don't like it here, wish I was back on the coast. If I am lucky something will turn up. It is just hurry up and wait. Here's hoping I see you soon.
Lots of Love,
Bob
P.S. I would give anything in the world to get out of this jail. Remember I love you more and more.

March 29, 1944
Dear Kitty,
They sure keep us busy. We have a schedule we keep. We go to
class at 8:00 to 5:30 and we haven't much time.

Last nite we had to roll our field packs and be ready by 8
in the morning. Keep our uniforms clean and pressed and if
we use our guns we have to clean them at night too so there is
always something to do. But I will always find time to write
. . .

I am writing this letter in a hurry because I have to clean
my gun, polish shoes, pack the pack again and make my bed
and take a shower. They don't give us much time for ourselves.
It is rush in and out as fast as we can. It is still the bunk. I
wish I was out of this mess.
Lots of Love,
Bob

During basic training, Papa was assigned as a weapons
mechanic. This necessitated another ten weeks of training in
disassembling, repairing, and reassembling everything from the
massive .57-caliber antitank gun to the M1s carried by enlisted
men.

March 26, 1944
Dear Kitty,
We were called out for a special training and sent up on top
to a hill about 12 miles from Fort MacArthur. We will have
7 weeks basic training and then have special training for 10
weeks. You see you are never stationary. As much as I know
now that I am going to be a company mechanic . . . I was too

homesick yesterday, I felt like crying but managed not to. I was standing in line and the sergeant came by and said I had my thoughts 100 miles away. I told him 1800 miles and he would be right. . . .

I am always thinking of you and when I am going to get out of this mess. I am telling you, it is just the same as being in jail. . . .

Boy I wish I was home. I sure do miss you miss you. I said it double but I mean it a thousand times. Everybody feels the same, too.

What shall I do. I will write you as much as I can. I don't know what's coming but I will not fail to write everyday.

Lots of Love, Bob

Basic training and the looming specter of war weren't the only things that concerned the men in the Army; they also had to worry about their wives and sweethearts back home. My grandfather couldn't have been happy when he heard about the working conditions for his wife.

May 3, 1944

Darling Bob,

This bunch down here at Cannon's is nearly as bad as you describe the bunch in the Army. Honestly, this class of fellows that they have down here is certainly low, and I don't mean perhaps. I get so disgusted with them sometimes that I could scream. They have no more office manners than a man in the moon. Yesterday, I was working on my producto board and Les came up and put his arm around me. Boy, it didn't take me very long to put it right off either. I can't stand anyone's

*arm around me except for yours, darling. Some of these fellows just cannot keep their hands off. It is really disgusting, isn't it? But you needn't worry. You know that don't you?
With all my love and kisses,
Kitty*

Fortunately, she sent another, more reassuring, letter in the evening, describing all the people who worked in her office, including herself, in a letter modeled after a gossip column:

*May 3, 1944
Kathleen Cozean: The "red-headed" secretary to Dale Parker. Her husband is in the army—a major or something. The wolves had better stay away from her—the only man she wants to see is her husband. I think his name is Bob, and from what she says he is a model husband.*

During his training, Papa was singled out and approached with the opportunity to join Officer Candidate School and continue training to become a lieutenant. He turned down the offer, unwilling to sign up for a four-year commitment, even though it would have delayed his trip to the front lines. Papa and Kitty were focused on their future together after the war. She resisted the urge to drop everything and follow him to training camp, and he turned down a chance to stay safely in additional training. After a few short months of training he boarded a troopship, bound for the front lines. But not without one more letter from his wife that contained a little extra . . . encouragement:

April 17, 1944
Darling Bob,
*Enclosing herewith is a "pin up" picture. You know you
wanted one so here it is. It was drawn by Bud Fouts, and
colored by your honorable wife—so. Hope you like it, but don't
bother telling anyone who sent it. I thought you might like it.*
Kitty

Unfortunately, the pin-up picture was the one thing that the
two of them didn't save.

On June 22, 1941, Hitler made a mistake that would prove to be
the undoing of the Third Reich—he attacked the Soviet Union.
He was concerned about the military power of the USSR and
ideologically opposed to communism. In attacking his former
ally, Hitler was attempting to eliminate them as a military threat
to his dominance of Europe. The German offensive easily cut
through Soviet lines, inflicting casualties that would have been
catastrophic to any other country in the war. Within six months
the Axis forces had driven to the gates of Stalingrad and Leningrad, two of the most important cities in the Soviet Union.

The attack on the Soviet Union required nearly 75 percent
of Germany's forces. It neutralized the threat of an invasion and
saved England from being the sole target of the Third Reich.
By holding the cities of Stalingrad and Leningrad, the Soviets
continued to occupy the majority of the manpower of the Axis,
allowing the British a much-needed respite until the United
States joined the fight.

It is important to understand—especially for my generation, half a century removed from the war and exposed since birth to Elie Wiesel's novels, *Schindler's List,* and the Holocaust Museum—that the young men on their way to the front lines weren't riding off on a quest to save the Jews and avenge Hitler's atrocities. In 1944, the horrors of Auschwitz and Bergen-Belsen were still unknown. Only vague rumors about the plight of the Jews, gypsies, homosexuals, and handicapped were heard, too hideous to be easily believed. But they had seen the Third Reich armies roll through Poland, Denmark, Belgium, the Netherlands, Luxembourg, France, Norway, Yugoslavia, Greece, Lithuania, Latvia, Estonia, Byelorussia, and the Ukraine, and had witnessed the devastation of the Japanese attack on Pearl Harbor. The men in training were angry over the American blood spilt in the Hawaiian Islands and determined to stop the spread of the Nazis. When I asked Papa why the men of his generation went to war, his answer was simple. "We didn't go to war to save the Jews. We went to kill Hitler."

With the Third Reich in control of all of Western Europe, getting onto the continent to kill Hitler and end the war appeared nearly impossible, even with the majority of German forces engaged on the Eastern Front against Russia. Allied command decided that an overwhelming assault on the beaches of France, across the English Channel, was the most direct and effective way to reach the heart of Germany. Unfortunately for our soldiers, Hitler's commanders were also aware of the importance of the beaches of Normandy.

By 1944 Germans had controlled France for four years and had used that time to make the beaches a killing field. The coastal waters contained more than six million mines and underwater obstacles. The cliffs above the beach were crisscrossed with concrete bunkers housing guns, antitank weapons, and artillery, all arranged to provide clear fields of fire at the men helplessly exiting the landing craft. Hitler had put his most trusted general, Field Marshal Erwin Rommel—the famous "Desert Fox"—in charge of the fortifications. Rommel was convinced the only chance for German success was to prevent the Allied forces from making the landing.

Field Marshal Rommel is one of the more fascinating characters in military history. His career began in World War I, when he fought in France, Romania, and Italy. Wounded in battle three times, he gained a reputation as both a great tactician and a brave soldier and was awarded Prussia's highest honor for valor. In Italy, he was caught behind enemy lines and managed to fight free, although almost all of his staff were captured or killed. The book he wrote analyzing the battles he had participated in during World War I, *Infantry Attacks,* became required reading for the leadership of both the Germans and the Allies. (It also prompted the enduring quote in *Patton,* Papa's favorite movie. "Rommel, you magnificent bastard," Patton cries when he first faces the Desert Fox in battle, "I read your book!")

During World War II, Rommel was involved in as much of the major fighting as any commander in the war. His first assignment was serving as the Fuhrer's personal escort service during the invasion of Poland. He guarded Hitler during the advance, spending a great deal of time with him as they toured the battlefield successes of the German Army. Rommel then asked for command of an armored division, a request immediately granted, to the envy of many other officers. Rommel soon validated Hitler's trust in the invasion of France. His division became known as the Ghost Division, advancing so far and so quickly that even the German High Command often didn't know exactly where they were. In France, the Ghost Division took two hundred miles in a single day, by far the longest such thrust in the war. It was also Rommel who was poised to attack the retreating British and French forces at the beaches of Dunkirk, though he was ordered to hold his position. As the first commander to reach the beach at the English Channel, it was appropriate that he would be the one tasked to defend those same beaches from the Allied invasion only a few years later—overseeing perhaps the greatest victory and most important defeat of Nazi Germany.

Rommel became renowned in Germany for his highly publicized victories in France and Africa, but he was also respected by the Allies for his humane treatment of prisoners and conquered foes. In the months after D-Day, he was accused of participating in the plan to assassinate Hitler. Because of Rommel's popularity in Germany, however, Hitler did not want his part in the plot coming to light. He sent two of his highest ranking generals to Rommel with a choice—he could be publically tried by the courts and executed, or choose to quietly commit suicide. If he was convicted, his staff would also be arrested and his family reduced to poverty, but if he chose to take the cyanide pill his staff would be spared and his family would receive his full military pension. After a few private moments of thought Rommel agreed, said goodbye to his wife and child, and got into a car with the two generals and a driver. It was reported in Germany that Rommel had died of injuries resulting from his staff car being strafed. A national day of mourning for the Desert Fox was instituted, and he was buried with full military honors. However, Rommel's distaste for the Nazis proved so strong that in his will he specified that his casket should be unadorned with any political symbols, an attempt to keep the swastika off his coffin. The truth about Rommel's death didn't come out until after the war, when one of the generals who had visited Rommel told the story at the Nuremberg trials.

One of Papa's favorite historical figures, Rommel was the example that he used when I asked why he didn't hate the Germans for all they had done. He simply replied, "they're just people, just like us. Some good, some bad." My grandfather thought of Rommel, and many of the Germans who fought for the Third Reich, as good men trapped on the wrong side of history.

While Papa was suffering through basic training and preparing to cross the Atlantic, Allied commanders were mustering forces and planning the attack on Rommel's fortifications. The largest amphibious assault ever launched, it would consist of two parts—the invasion of the German-held coastline with overwhelming Allied strength, and a paratrooper attack the night before the landing to slow any counterattack. The plan, code-named Operation Overlord, was set for June 6, 1944. D-Day.

Preceding the invasion, British and American paratroopers dropped from the night sky behind enemy lines. A night jump was a risky tactic that had never been used before, and would never be used again in World War II. The men jumped from the planes knowing that if the invasion failed, they would be cut off behind enemy lines in occupied France, almost certain to be captured or killed. However, their primary mission—to facilitate the landing and slow any German counterattack on the vulnerable landing troops—was vital to the invasion. Allied paratroopers attacked and destroyed artillery that covered the beaches, captured bridges, and cut communication lines despite the dangers.

Many men were scattered by the night jump, lost and unable to form up with their units in the darkness. They banded together in small groups, attacking whatever targets they could and hampering the German response to the invasion and achieving their primary objective.

As the paratroopers began sabotaging German roads and communications, over seven thousand ships from eight different countries steamed toward a fifty-mile stretch of Normandy beaches. More than 160,000 men would pour off the troop transports into the shallow Atlantic water off the coast of France on June 6, walking straight into the withering fire of German machine guns, which were positioned on the cliffs above the beach. The convoy was heavily protected by planes, warships, and minefields from German naval attack. Guided by airplanes and observers on the beaches, the warships off the coast provided covering fire, lobbing huge shells onto the German defenses. Still, even that firepower failed to prevent the water from turning red with the blood of Allied soldiers.

The size and scope of this invasion is almost impossible to grasp. If the 160,000 men who surged out of the landing craft on D-Day were lined up shoulder to shoulder, their line would encompass all fifty miles of the Normandy beaches they attacked. I have visited the memorial at Omaha Beach and stood on the tall cliffs overlooking the white sand. The Germans stood on those cliffs as they fired into the onrushing troops, packed so closely together in the shallow water a bullet could hardly miss. Men, most younger than me, spilled out of the landing craft into the killing fields to establish a beachhead. Atop the cliffs is a cemetery, lined with rows of white crosses, that shows the true cost of the victory.

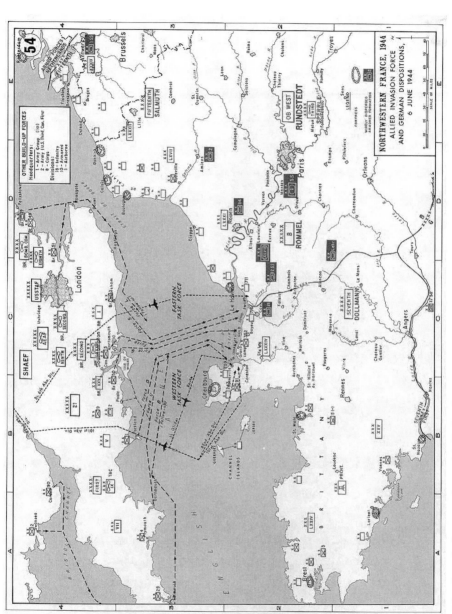

Map, from the American Army, of the D-Day Invasion

The attack on the beaches of Normandy on D-Day, despite heavy casualties, was ultimately successful, allowing the full power of the Allied forces to pour through into Europe. It would be the beginning of the end of the Third Reich. When they announced to my grandfather and the rest of the troops training at Camp Fannin that the Allied had landed at Omaha Beach, the ranks broke into cheers and clapping.

Kitty wrote my grandfather that evening, hopeful the Allied success would keep her husband out of the war:

June 6, 1944
Darling Bob,
Well, darling, it is here—THE INVASION—isn't that wonderful? Golly, I can hardly believe it, but guess it is really true this time. This morning when I got the paper, there it was—INVASION—in great big letters across the headlines.

Guess that is all we will hear about today. Maybe instead of just a furlough in July, you can come home to stay.

Well, darling, I know this is a short letter, but it is time to go to work so will close and write more tonight.
With all my love and kisses,
Kitty
P.S. Keep your chin up sweets and you'll be home before you know it. Just hope I will be able to line up to your expectations. I'll try awfully hard.

After breaking through Rommel's defenses onto the European continent at the beaches of Normandy, Allied forces rapidly advanced into France and Belgium, driving the overextended German armies backward. Supplies lagged behind the Allies, stuck in a bottleneck on the beaches they had stormed months earlier. Gasoline and ammunition were in especially short supply as the army advanced. The German army was overextended and giving ground, fighting against the Russians in the east and the British and American armies in the west. Hitler felt his sole chance for victory in the two-front war was to somehow neutralize the threat in the west so that he could deal with his enemies separately. He ordered a counterattack, hoping to split the American and British lines and encircle their armies. A massive defeat, he reasoned, might force them to sue for peace, leaving the German army free to concentrate on the Russians advancing from the east. These orders were received and passed through the German command as my grandfather was sent up to the front.

Papa's first view of Europe was from a combat truck rattling through France and Belgium on its way to the front lines of World War II. It had been more than nine months since he kissed Kitty goodbye, first for basic training and then for the trip across the Atlantic to fight Hitler and the armies of the Third Reich.

My grandfather and his fellow soldiers were dropped off in the thick woods of Belgium, opposite the German Army that had been driven back from the coast of France—the same woods that had been so disastrous for the French Army when Hitler invaded. There was two feet of snow on the ground, and every breath was visible in the winter chill. The men wore every stich of clothing they had in the sleeping bags to try and stay warm. One man who left his boots on the ground woke up the next morning to find them frozen solid.

After reaching the front, they and the rest of the 106th Division relieved the troops who had been dug in and fighting since D-Day. I can only imagine the scene; my grandfather's company, freshly laundered and clean-shaven, spilling from the truck, shocked at the sight of the weary soldiers who had been marching and fighting throughout Europe. My grandfather and several other men were ordered forward, a few hundred yards in front of the main line, to serve as forward scouts. Bunkering down into foxholes or under pine trees on the snowy ground, arranging their grenades and rifles, they didn't have to wait long for their first glimpse of war.

Around midnight Papa heard the diesel engines of the German trucks starting up, an ominous growl drifting across the chilly night air. All they could do was check the position of their guns and the proximity of the hand grenades lining the foxholes. A few hours later bullets began to whiz over their heads in the pre-dawn gloom, and they scrambled out of their sleeping bags, retreating to rejoin the main line and warn of the attack. As they crossed an open field, German mortar shells began to rain down. Sixty-six years later, my grandfather described the scene to me with an almost eerie detachment, recalling dispassionately the "arms and legs falling off and all that." They were caught in the forefront of the final German offensive of World War II, what came to be called the Battle of the Bulge. With more than eight hundred thousand men engaged, it was America's largest and bloodiest battle of the war.

Regrouping into a copse of trees for shelter from the hail of bombs and shrapnel, the firing stopped, and quiet descended for the first time since the sun had risen. The men were excited, believing that the Germans had been killed, captured, or run away—until they saw American troops walking out with their hands over their heads.

I was surprised to hear that my grandfather and his company weren't informed that they were surrendering. Papa just laughed. "Who would have told us?"

Upon seeing fellow American soldiers surrendering, the men destroyed their weapons by breaking the stock, dismantling them, and tossing the important bits in different directions to keep their guns out of enemy hands. When I asked what my grandfather thought about having to destroy his rifle without firing a shot, he gave an honest answer. "Well, I hate to admit it, but there just wasn't anyone to shoot at."

The men left the treeline with their hands in the air and followed the line of captured Americans. When they reached the road, a German soldier shoved my grandfather to the ground and bellowed something in his native tongue. On the side of a muddy road, with the muzzle of a Nazi rifle in his face, all the rumors of German brutality toward prisoners flooded his mind and Papa was convinced that he was about to be murdered.

CHAPTER 3

Diagnosed

AFTER OUR CONVERSATION ON THANKSGIVING NIGHT, I DECIDED that I needed to hear about Papa's experience in its entirety. Hearing only his scattered stories, it was impossible to imagine the German POW camp of his tales. When I asked him that night if I could come up to Pasadena to interview him, listen to him tell the story from start to finish, the only reaction I got was a small, almost imperceptible smile. But he was clearly excited, and soon all his friends and the rest of the family knew that his grandson was going to be interviewing him.

Several months passed, and life got in the way of my resolution. Sick of stingy customers and the smell of barbecue sauce oozing out of my pores, I had quit the restaurant where I waited tables. I went to work full-time with my mother, who runs several small medical device and pharmaceutical companies. Surprisingly, I turned out to be pretty good at it. I was putting my degree to use, designing medical devices, writing grant proposals, and working on regulatory submissions with the Food and Drug Administration. Everything was run from the home office, which meant no commute, a fully stocked kitchen, and a break room with a big screen TV. And, best of all, I was able to work my own hours, which seldom involved much movement before noon.

Just a month after I promised to interview Papa, I headed back to Kenya, my fourth trip to Africa in the last three years, with the East Africa Partnership (EAP). When I first got involved, the EAP was focused on providing clean drinking water and a few college scholarships, but it was growing rapidly. We added new programs, including a much-needed medical program, and built several orphanages.

Though my first trip had been primarily motivated by the opportunity for an all-expense-paid vacation to exotic Africa and my desire to see the world, I found that I enjoyed working with the people in Kenya. While I had travelled extensively before my first trip to Africa, there is a world of difference between visiting as a tourist and working as part of a mission team. I was stunned by the poverty we saw in Kenya, but even more overwhelmed by the joy, generosity, and faith of the people we met there. I began looking forward to the next trip, drawn back by both the people we had met and the sense of accomplishment at trip's end. For three weeks, I could be the person that I wanted to be—caring, confident, selfless, devoted to helping others. Those trips were intermissions from "real" life, and I always came back focused, with a fresh perspective and gratitude for the blessings that I take for granted.

Over the next two years I went back four times. The first trips were spent doing traditional mission work—laying the foundation for the orphanage, constructing a home for a local pastor, repainting a church—but I soon started working with the doctors and nurses as we did our first medical trips. Travelling to remote dispensaries on roads that were more pothole than surface, we would find hundreds of patients waiting for us when we arrived, many having walked for several days to be treated. The team would set up, each doctor or nurse finding a room, free corner of a church, or a shaded place under a tree where patients could be seen. They would be sent to the pharmacy for medication, and the line would often have more than a hundred patients waiting patiently for their prescriptions. I began helping out there, at first only counting pills, but soon learning the proper dosages and durations of treatment for all the conditions we were seeing.

On this trip I had been appointed as the leader of the medical team. Our focus was on treating handicapped children, who are seen in many places in Africa as cursed and confined inside the home. We were hoping, with the help of the local churches, to try and overturn that stereotype.

On this trip I came home with more baggage than I had left with—I had managed to find myself a girlfriend. Nicole was the physical therapist on my team, and we got to know each other while working together. I didn't think I had much of a chance with her, since she was five years older than I was and way out of my league in the looks department, but I was aided by the fact that just about anyone can start looking good after three weeks in Africa. And I was the only unattached male on the trip, which I'm sure helped. As I like to say, if you give me three weeks in Africa with no competition, I'm pretty much irresistible.

In the midst of all these changes, it was difficult to visit Papa and interview him about his time as a POW. With the faith of a boy in his grandfather, I was sure he was indestructible and I would have plenty of time with him. Nicole, who works with a lot of elderly patients, urged me to make the time, saying, prophetically, that there is a very thin line between a person that age being completely healthy and being very sick. Even if they seem to be doing great, a small setback can often be tough to overcome.

A few short months later, as if on cue, Papa began struggling to catch his breath. We noticed that his face was losing color, turning an ashen shade. He was diagnosed with a faulty heart valve, which was causing the breathing problems and which the doctors told us could kill him at any time. He had two options: submit to open-heart surgery to repair the valve and suffer through the recovery period afterward, or gradually decline until the valve finally gave out and his heart stopped. Given the new-found urgency, I braved Los Angeles traffic and made the drive to his house, perched above a busy, oak-lined street, and climbed the steep brick steps to his door with pen and notebook in hand.

He had designed and built the house himself in the summer of 1947, after finishing his military duty. The blueprints that he had drawn to scale were tucked away in the back corner of a closet. He enlisted his friends and together they dug out the side of a hill, planning to go deeper until an encounter with solid bedrock changed their minds, leaving the house high above the street below and necessitating a driveway that was probably the steepest in Southern California. The house combined amazing craftsmanship in the hardwood floors and arched ceilings with the quirks that you only get when you build a house yourself.

After finishing construction with the washer and dryer in the basement, Papa quickly tired of tromping down the stairs with his dirty clothes every day. Realizing the only thing standing between him and the laundry room below was the floor, he found the only logical solution—he cut a hole in it. Resting in the bathroom and disguised with a cabinet built over it, the hole allowed him to pull back the bottom "drawer" and drop his clothes directly into the washing machine, open and waiting below. In the basement a room sat empty for thirteen years, awaiting the pool table that he had always coveted but couldn't afford until 1960. In the back corner was the woodshop, a cacophony of wood scraps and rusting tools, with nails and screws securely deposited in aluminum tins from companies that had gone out of business decades before.

Because I had begun the process of buying my own house, I paid more attention to the house than usual as I parked and walked up the steps. I had spent the prior several weeks touring Orange County with a real estate agent, looking at different places. My price range was still on the low end for California, and just about every house we visited was somewhere between rundown and dilapidated, making my appreciation for Papa's craftsmanship even greater.

Papa was slightly out of breath when he opened the thick oak door, but was excited to see me. After I gave him a hug he quickly disappeared, returning with a thick binder, falling apart and overflowing with old telegrams, photographs, documents, and newspaper clippings. It hit the kitchen table with a weighty thud, and we sat in silence for a few long seconds—I guess I was expecting the pent-up story to spill out unprompted. Idly I flipped open the binder, slowly turning the fragile pages. Papa broke the silence, pointing out documents and letters as we eased into the interview.

I spent the rest of the morning walking a fine line, trying to avoid questions that were painful or embarrassing while still getting the details of a haunting experience. I was surprised that it was difficult to get him to open up. Because he spent so much time telling his stories to anyone who would listen, I had assumed that I would be able to ask a few simple questions and get him talking. During the course of the interview, I realized that the stories he told were the stories he wanted to tell. To get the whole experience, I would have to probe with questions I wasn't comfortable asking and he wasn't comfortable answering. Many of them garnered no more than a yes or a no, or even just a nod.

As a result, interviewing him was exhausting. I had to ask my grandfather what it was like to see a friend cut in half by machine gun fire, what it was like to feel his body waste away. I had to ask if he ever lost hope of being rescued and returning to his wife. It must have been even more difficult for him, having to relive that time with his grandson—not just the few stories he had honed with retelling, but the entire raw experience. There were long pauses after many of my questions, as he struggled with his memories and the emotional weight they still carried. As we pored over the documents he had placed in his binder—a map of the POW camps, the Western Union telegrams that his wife had received from the Department of War, pictures he had taken in Paris, the Red Cross POW card that he had sent from the prison camp—our eyes rarely met.

Even as I learned about what Papa had been through, I began to lose something else. Gone was my blind hero worship. When he was shipped off to fight Hitler, he had been just a kid struggling to become a man and get his life on track. I knew the feeling. As we got up from the table, his eyes met mine, and he got in the last question. "Do you think you would have survived?" I didn't have an answer.

In the camp Papa learned to survive on his own, and when he got home there was no one he could share his experiences with. Unless you had been there, as he stressed often that morning, you couldn't possibly understand. At least I knew the general feeling—it was something I had strongly experienced after returning from Africa for the first time, and something we warned others about in our meetings before new trips left. People tried taking photographs, shooting video, or scribbling extensive notes in diaries, but ultimately their friends and relatives back home would never truly understand. Even his country didn't know how to think of those who had been taken prisoner. After all, there is little glamour or glory in a prisoner of war camp. Almost universally, the former POWs kept their experiences bottled up. Many, like Papa, began opening up to their friends and families only years later. Others refused to revisit the pain of those dark times at all; Papa had called men he knew from the camp who still would not speak of their time in Stalag IXB, even with one of their own. But the connection between those former POWs was vital—the only people who could really understand were those who had been through it together.

After spending the morning talking about his time as a prisoner of war, we went out to lunch. I was certainly ready for the break. Fittingly, we went to Sizzler. This time I was the one driving as we headed down the streets to the restaurant. Fortunately, the menu at Sizzler never changes, so at least that remained constant; chicken wings, chocolate mousse, and sickly sweet ice cream covered with butterscotch syrup and heaping scoops of sprinkles were still available.

He was quiet as we ate, staring at his food. I thought it was because of all the memories we had dredged up that morning, but

I was wrong. It was the Tuesday after Labor Day, and it marked the first time in fifty-two years he hadn't been able to visit his cabin in the San Bernardino Mountains. The men in my family are all characterized—or cursed—by an unnatural consistency: Papa visits the mountains every Labor Day, my father has never been late or called in sick to work in thirty years, and all three of us start each day off with a hearty bowl of Wheaties, the Breakfast of Monotony, with a half-spoon of sprinkled sugar. This year his doctor had strictly prohibited a trip to the cabin, afraid that his heart, already overworked, wouldn't be able to handle the strain of the thin mountain air.

The faulty heart valve that would eventually necessitate his second open-heart surgery had robbed him of his vitality. Unable to get enough air or catch his breath, he had been forced to slowly give up his golf game (again characterized by consistency—he drives the ball eighty yards and dead straight, regardless of whether the hole is fifty or five hundred yards away), vacations, and finally his tradition of aromatic pines, mountain roads, and swatting golf balls off his back porch. Not much speaks to Papa's mischievous nature like seeing him check over both shoulders for witnesses before teeing off down into the deep empty canyon below. The first time I got to participate in this curiously exhilarating ritual instead of being the lookout, he handed me a left-handed club, assuring me it would be fine when I awkwardly hefted it and looked at him questioningly. Of course, it wasn't—I hooked the ball so badly I missed the canyon altogether, and it landed on a neighbor's deck with a heart-stopping thump. Quickly checking to make sure the coast was clear, Papa gave me a boost over the gate to retrieve the evidence.

At our nostalgia-inducing lunch I saw my grandfather as an old man for the first time, betrayed by his body. His energy and vitality, tennis matches, golfing excursions, and games of pool, had masked the inexorable progression of age, at least to me. How frustrating it must be to work your whole life with your hands to provide for a family, to grow up in the Great Depression and survive a prison camp in the most costly war in the history of the world, only to find yourself gasping for breath after a trip to the bathroom.

The hesitation in his voice as he asked for my advice let me know how apprehensive he was about submitting himself to the surgeon's scalpel. He didn't share my blind faith in his immortality. The surgeon had already explained the procedure and assured him that there was a good chance of complete recovery, although the surgery itself could be fatal to a man in his condition. I gave Papa my honest opinion, reiterating the advice my parents had given, although I had to phrase it in the sports talk that we are comfortable with. I told him I thought he should swing for the fences.

It was the first adult conversation we had ever had. I'm not even sure if you would call it a conversation, but it was as close as we had ever gotten. Not for lack of love or time spent together, but maybe just because until then he hadn't seen me as anything more than a kid. Our interactions were either lectures from him about driving safely and studying hard, or vague "how-is-school-going" questions that are easily brushed aside. I'm not sure if, with this encounter, he was recognizing me as an adult, or if I was finally beginning to act like it, challenging him with my questions instead of passively listening to his stories as I had in the past.

Whether I was ready or not, the dynamic between us had changed. It was the first time he had ever asked for my help, and the first time I had ever seen him afraid. Our relationship was deeper, but I already missed the child-grandfather roles that we had left behind in our conversation about his experiences in Germany. I could tell he felt it too as I helped him up from the sticky vinyl booth and, for the first time, paid for lunch.

CHAPTER 4

The Boxcar

As soon as possible after their capture, prisoners of war shall be evacuated to depots sufficiently removed from the fighting zone for them to be out of danger. Only prisoners who, by reason of their wounds or maladies, would run greater risks by being evacuated than by remaining may be kept temporarily in a dangerous zone. Prisoners shall not be unnecessarily exposed to danger while awaiting evacuation from a fighting zone. The evacuation of prisoners on foot shall in normal circumstances be effected by stages of not more than 20 kilometres per day, unless the necessity for reaching water and food depôts requires longer stages.

—ARTICLE 7, GENEVA CONVENTION, SIGNED BY GERMANY ON JULY 7TH, 1929

Dec 24: Got bombed in railroad yard. Cars bounce like match boxes.

—ROBERT COZEAN, PRISON DIARY, 1944

THE GERMAN SOLDIER RIPPED THE BACKPACK FROM MY GRAND-father's shoulders and threw it into the ditch on the side of the road. Papa had forgotten to remove his bayonet from the pack, and now he was forced to leave it behind. German tanks trundled past as the prisoners marched down the side of the road, followed closely by trucks with the famous Red Cross emblazoned on the side loaded with ammunition and additional fuel. Prisoners who were too badly wounded to walk were thrown across the tanks, lying on the cold steel until they reached a hospital. German soldiers, headed to the front, paused to snatch watches, rings, overcoats, or even shoes from the captured men—anything that caught their eye.

The prisoners marched for four days from Belgium into Germany, receiving food and water only once, surviving by eating snow off the ground. The column covered more than thirty kilometers (nineteen miles) per day. My grandfather only remembers sleeping for a few hours in an abandoned church in Prum, Germany. Injured men were treated by captured American medical personnel, using whatever bandages and medication they were carrying when they surrendered. When the exhausted prisoners reached a rail depot, they were steered, like so many cattle, onto a boxcar for a trip deeper into the heart of Germany. The boxcars were ubiquitous on the railroad tracks in Germany, ferrying soldiers, ammunition, and supplies to the front. They were called Forty and Eights, because of their ability to carry either forty men or eight horses.

Papa and sixty other men pressed shoulder to shoulder in the car, standing or sitting on the dirty straw with their knees by their ears, too crowded to even extend their legs. The American intelligence report shows that they spent five days, including Christmas Day, in the boxcar. Eight men tried to escape, prying open the barbed wire from the sole window and leaping from the car into a field, where they were killed by an exploding land mine. A

German guard, enraged by the escape attempt, began shooting wildly into the boxcars, killing another American captive.

Hunger and thirst soon became unbearable for the trapped prisoners. They had been captured on December 17, forced to march by the bayonets of German guards for four days, and loaded onto a boxcar too crowded to lie down in for five more and only given water once. Some of the men still had a few supplies from their packs or canteens they had secreted inside their jackets, but my grandfather was left with nothing after losing his pack. As he later shared, in a typically understated manner, "They say you can live ten days without water, but I didn't want to test it."

Two days after the prisoners boarded the train, Allied planes bombed the railroad yard where the boxcar was parked. The Germans didn't give any indication that prisoners were in the cars, and rail yards were often targeted to disrupt the German war effort. Shoulder to shoulder in the boxcar, the men cushioned each other as the bombs shook the train on its tracks. Locked in the car and helpless, there was nothing the prisoners could do but pray the American pilots would miss. The captives in my grandfather's car emerged with only bruises, but many others were not as fortunate.

The only free space in the boxcar was reserved for the corner piss-bucket. As will happen when sixty men use one bucket, it filled rapidly, and a few soldiers came up with an ingenious plan to empty it. They waited until the train began to slow, coming into a station. A man at the front of the car signaled the men by the bucket, who emptied the contents out the window—directly onto a German guard at the station.

The timing was precise, but the guard reacted the way you would expect a man with a gun to react to a bucket of urine cascading over his face. As the train slowed to a stop he raised his rifle and yelled *"Rause! Rause!"* "Out! Out!" But, just as the men began to fearfully file out of the car, an older German officer with a flowing handlebar mustache looked at the furious young guard and merely raised his hand. Perhaps he was a good man, showing mercy to captured enemies. Perhaps he didn't want to deal with the paperwork and cleanup resulting from a young hothead opening fire into a group of unarmed prisoners in retribution for a face-full of bodily waste. I'd like to think he stopped the guard because it was pretty damn funny and his handlebar mustache was hiding a smirk. Whatever the reason, the prisoners were ordered to reboard the boxcar.

After the train chugged out of the station and the tension eased, a man called out, "Can we all laugh now?" Laughter filled the boxcar as it trundled deeper into Germany, headed for Stalag IXB. Papa said it was the last time he laughed for four months.

~⌐~

When Germany invaded Czechoslovakia in 1939, the army began searching for sites where prison camps could be easily constructed. The locations had to be flat with good visibility to ensure the construction of the camp would be as inexpensive as possible and to reduce any possibility for escape. Moreover, the surrounding land needed was supposed to be arable and capable of producing good crops, which the prisoners could cultivate. The plot of land also needed to be large enough to hold up to ten thousand prisoners, and water had to be readily available. Finally, the location needed to be removed from main routes of traffic, but less than five kilometers from a railroad depot to facilitate the arrival of prisoners. Stalag IXB, intended to be only a transfer station,

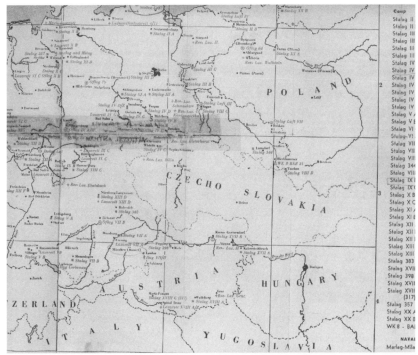

Map of the German POW camps made by the Red Cross and given to Papa.

was much smaller than most of the other prison camps and was already severely overcrowded when Papa arrived.

Over the course of the war, ninety-five thousand Americans fell into German hands and were scattered throughout fifty-four prison camps. The first large capture of American prisoners occurred in North Africa in November of 1942, while the Allies were fighting Rommel. Their invasion of Italy in 1943 also cost them many captured personnel, and isolated pockets of men were forced to surrender in June of 1944 in the battle for the beaches at Normandy.

As the war progressed and the bombing runs over Germany intensified, the number of captured airmen increased. In general, the conditions at the camps for pilots and crews were much better than those for the infantry. They were run by the Luftwaffe and generally conformed to the rules of the Geneva Convention. However, surviving to be captured wasn't always easy for the airplane crews. First they had to escape their crippled plane and parachute down, often at night. Then, after drifting to earth, the downed pilots often found themselves at the mercy of German civilians, who lived under constant threat of death from above, a fear fueled by Nazi propaganda. Often the German populace took vengeance upon the pilots who landed in their villages, and many airmen didn't survive to be captured.

But by far the greatest number of troops to surrender came during the Battle of the Bulge, where Papa was captured. Caught completely by surprise by the German counterattack, more than twenty-three thousand American soldiers were taken captive and marched to prison camps, including four thousand in a single day. Like my grandfather, many of the surrendering troops were fresh reinforcements, encircled and trapped in their first military action. Others were veterans of the D-Day landings, exhausted from six months of constant fighting across Europe. The prisoners were divided up and sent to different camps, depending on their rank. Stalag IXB was only for enlisted men.

Prisoners were supposed to be treated according to the Geneva Convention, an international treaty created in 1929 and ratified by almost every country that later participated in World War II. Only the USSR and Japan had not signed, although Japan agreed to treat its POWs according to the rules of the Convention. The document required that POWs be given food, clothing, and shelter comparable to the country's own troops. Adequate medical care was to be provided. Receipts would be given for any money or valuables taken from the prisoner, and long, forced marches of captured troops would be prohibited. Papa's treatment at Stalag IXB would violate every one of these rules.

The boxcar came to a stop in the late afternoon. My grandfather and the other men spilled out, many collapsing to the ground when they no longer had the support of the men crowded around them. Clinging together for strength and encouragement, the prisoners staggered two miles on cobblestone streets to the outskirts of a German town, where they reached the gates of the prison camp where they would spend the rest of the war.

Stalag IXB was located outside Bad Orb, a spa and holiday town in northern Germany. Far enough from the front lines to be untouched by the war, the narrow streets, old-fashioned lampposts, and steeply gabled, snow-covered buildings would seem quaint and cozy under better circumstances. The citizens stared at my grandfather and the other Americans as they limped and stumbled through the town.

The camp itself was built on eighty-five acres of land, set in the middle of an untouched pine forest. Before the war it had been a holiday camp, but a grim silence had replaced children's laughter. Originally designed as a transfer station, where prisoners would be briefly held before being shipped off to other camps around the country, the camp had not been intended to permanently house POWs. My grandfather and the 984 other soldiers captured in the first two days of the German counter-attack at the Battle of the Bulge were the first American soldiers to be interned at Stalag IXB. However, when they arrived there were already Russian, Serbian, and British captives housed within the walls, all separated by nationality and not allowed any contact. The British prisoners—captured at Dunkirk where they guarded the evacuation—had been POWs for more than three years when Papa and the Americans were herded through the front gates.

The perimeter of the compound was ringed with a barbed wire fence, which sat outside a smaller, low-slung fence and was topped with more ominous curls of barbed wire. Floodlights and guard towers were evenly spaced around the perimeter of the camp. The prisoners would learn that the area between the two fences was prohibited; any man who entered it would be shot on sight.

After entering they were given a bowl of thin potato soup—only their second taste of food since their capture more than eight days before. My grandfather was issued a blanket and POW dog tags inscribed with his new identity, #23781. It was the day after Christmas, December 26, 1944.

A few weeks later, on January 12, 1945, my grandmother Kathleen got the telegram from the secretary of war that families of the military have dreaded for generations: Her husband was missing in action.

WESTERN UNION

1201   (21)

The filing time shown in the date line on telegrams and day letters is STANDARD TIME at point of origin. Time of receipt is STANDARD TIME at point of destination

SAM69 44 GOVT=WUX WASHINGTON DC 12 537P

1945 JAN 12 PM 3 23

MRS KATHLEEN M COZEAN

=109 EAST AVE 45=

THE SECRETARY OF WAR DESIRES ME TO EXPRESS HIS DEEP REGRET
THAT YOUR HUSBAND PRIVATE FIRST CLASS ROBERT P COZEAN HAS
BEEN REPORTED MISSING IN ACTION SINCE SIXTEEN DECEMBER IN
GERMANY IF FURTHER DETAILS OR OTHER INFORMATION ARE RECEIVED
YOU WILL BE PROMPTLY NOTIFIED=
=DUNLOP ACTING THE ADJUTANT GENERAL.

The notice from the Secretary of War informing Kitty that her husband was missing in action after being sent to the front lines.

Our sympathy for trying times of suspense to Mrs. Robert P. Cozean and Mr. and Mrs. W. B. Cozean because of the report that Robert P. Cozean is missing action. Our prayer is that he will soon be found safe, possibly as a prisoner of Germany.

The article in the local paper, saved by Kitty, after the news arrived.

Chapter 5

Surgery

I HAD ALWAYS THOUGHT THAT ANYONE WHO SAID THEY "COULD hardly recognize him" was being, at best, melodramatic. Then I visited Papa in the hospital after his surgery. Entering a private room, I saw a sick old man in a paper-thin gown lying in the bed. His eyes were closed, his face was ashen, and his hair was wildly unkempt. The narrow hospital bed was surrounded by a riot of blinking and beeping machines, and he didn't stir when I walked in. A few get-well cards and a heart-shaped red pillow emblazoned with the USC Medical Center logo were the only things in the room. Stunned and confused, I turned and put my hand on the doorknob to leave, murmuring an apology. I paused for a second at the door and rechecked the number on the room, almost surprised when it matched the one given to me by the front desk.

As I finally recognized Papa, my eyes followed three blood-stained plastic tubes from a bucket on the floor up the side of the hospital bed and saw them disappear into his chest. As I watched, the blood-streaked fluid slowly trickled down through them. An IV line plunged into his hand, held there by clear tape, dripping antibiotics and nutrients directly into his bloodstream. A catheter slithered out from under the blankets, emptying into a urine basin attached to the bed. The automatic blood pressure cuff wrapped around his upper arm startled me, coming to life in a puff of compressed air. A bedside monitor beeped constantly with his changing pulse and oxygen levels. The entire effect was dehumanizing. I hadn't lost a family member since my grandmother (on my mother's side) died of leukemia when I was only ten. I hadn't been allowed to visit her in the hospital, spared from seeing the effects of radiation and chemotherapy. When I saw Papa, I realized what a gift my grandmother gave me as a child by not letting me remember her as a patient in a hospital bed.

Before my grandfather's surgery, I had looked up exactly what the procedure he was undergoing entailed. He had just been through a valve replacement, changing out his aortic valve with a valve from a pig, just like a mechanic dropping in a new transmission. They used a sternal saw (nearly identical to the jigsaws sold in Home Depot) to cut through his eighty-eight-year-old breastbone and pulled his rib cage apart, exposing his heart. He was attached to a heart-lung machine, which does the work of both organs, so that the surgeons can work without the lungs and heart moving around. A potassium solution, the same type used to put convicts to death, stopped his heart, rendering him completely dependent on the machine to keep him alive for the remainder of the procedure. His heart was then opened up with a small, razor-sharp scalpel, slicing through the outer wall to allow them to replace an internal valve. During the operation, the surgeon also found and fixed a previously undiscovered hole in the mitral valve.

Scheduled for three hours, the surgery took seven. The doctors had trouble sewing up his sternum, as the bones were too weak to hold the rib cage together. The malfunctioning atrial valve had been causing the shortness of breath, weakness, and the inability to get enough oxygen into his body; the previously undiscovered hole in the mitral valve would have killed him.

It's amazing he even woke up. The time when he was supposed to be out of surgery came and went, the hours dragging on. Through all of it, I never really considered the possibility that he wouldn't emerge from the double doors of the operating room, even though his chances at that point were probably less than fifty-fifty. Despite how weak and vulnerable he looked in his hospital gown, I was still sure he would be hitting golf balls in the mountains again in a few months, when we could laugh together at how bad he had looked. It never occurred to me that this might be the beginning of the end.

My mother had accompanied Papa to the hospital and been with him as the anesthesiologist put him to sleep, his eyes closing as both of them wondered, separately, if they would open again. She and Papa had always been close, especially after the death of his wife. They talked on the phone several times a week until Papa's hearing began to fade and he was unable to hear her higher-pitched voice. She was waiting when he got out of the OR to hear the surgeon's report, and more importantly, to be with him when he woke. After opening his eyes and regaining his bearings, Papa's first words were accompanied by as much of a wry smile as he could muster: "I'm a survivor."

It had been several days since the surgery, but he still looked so fragile and helpless in bed I was afraid to touch him. When I warily rested my hand on his arm his eyes flickered open and darted around the room, and it took him several long moments to rasp out my name. I pulled a chair closer to the bed, sitting as far from the fluid-filled bucket on the floor as possible in the tight quarters.

After an hour or so together, the assistant surgeon came in and examined the bucket that the chest tubes were draining into. Evidently the flow of blood and fluid from the wounded area had slowed considerably, enough that they could safely remove the chest tubes. I got up to leave, but the doctor told me I could stay. And when Papa's eyes met mine I could see he was hoping I would. It was the first time I was in an uncomfortable medical situation with him, but it certainly wouldn't be the last. Reluctantly I watched as she told Papa to take a deep breath and let it out. As he exhaled she took the thickest tube in both hands and steadily pulled. His eyes opened wide as she continued to tug hand over hand—there was more of the tube in his chest than I thought was possible. After it was finally out, she gave him a moment to recover before moving on to the next tube and a few minutes later, the only evidence that remained were three neatly punched holes, between the size of a dime and a quarter, below his rib cage.

Even more than most patients, Papa hated the hospital. Spending a week in the ICU recovering, he missed the comfort, routine, and familiar clutter of his home. Lying in bed left him nothing to do. Never much of a reader, Papa's only sedentary pursuits were watching television and doing crossword puzzles, usually completed with the assistance of a library of crossword reference books, which he consulted for nearly every clue. Without his library, crossword puzzles were useless, and most of his time was spent trying to nap with the blood pressure cuff waking him every fifteen minutes.

Papa's only respite from the boredom was his visitors. As he improved, my dad drove up to visit after work nearly every day, braving the Los Angeles rush hour traffic to spend the evening hours by his father's bed. Over the two weeks of Papa's hospital stay, my dad was in his element, given something concrete to do, translating emotion into action. The same characteristic had seen him at every one of my basketball games, no matter how far away or terrible the competition. With the very real possibility of his father not surviving the surgery or being able to come home from the hospital, I think my dad was grateful to be able to help. And while I'm certain a fly on the wall would have been bored to tears by their conversation about the day's traffic or the Lakers' last game, I know how much it mattered to Papa. My mother would sometimes drive up to give my dad a break, and my great-aunt Ruthie and I would also visit to fill in empty days on the schedule. We worked hard to make sure that he got at least one visitor a day during his stay at the hospital.

This procedure was his third major surgery of the last decade, and after each one he came to live with my parents as he recovered. His house, with the slanted driveway and steep steps, was out of the question until he regained strength. The responsibility fell to my parents, both because of their proximity and because my uncle Keith had stepped away from our family and Papa when he converted to Mormonism.

About ten years earlier, doctors had detected blockages in the vessels surrounding Papa's heart. This led to his first open-heart surgery, a quintuple bypass. Veins were extracted from his legs and used to replace the damaged vessels in his chest. He was released only three days after that surgery, despite the fact his chest wound continued to ooze and the incisions on his legs were actively bleeding. I had just started high school, and it was my job to prepare for his arrival while my mother picked him up. I put a nice mattress on the pull-out couch downstairs, made the bed, and removed any potential obstacles from his path. I remember being stunned at how sick he looked when I had to help him out of the car, shouldering most of his weight as I helped him to bed.

As soon as he could sit up on his own, Papa started making the case that he was ready to go home. To stop his cajoling, my mother gave him the terms of his release—he had to demonstrate the ability to circumnavigate the house several times and climb up and down the stairs without resting or toppling over. After nearly a month of rehab, he passed the test and returned to his own home, going back to his independent and active life, although without egg yolks and with less bacon. Back on the par-3 golf course a few months later, he showed no lasting ill effects from the procedure, but did enjoy occasionally opening his shirt to showcase his impressive surgery scar.

Those same rules came in handy a few years later, when he had his aching left knee replaced. Papa actually spent longer in the hospital after his knee replacement than after the heart surgery, due to a bad reaction to the anesthesia. Eventually he was released and, after another rehab stint at my parents' house, headed home, soon forsaking the cane the doctor had recommended as his leg grew stronger.

So by the time Papa arrived at the house after his third surgery, we all knew the drill. His customary bed was made in the living room after I lugged the mattress down the stairs and laid it over the pull-out couch. A stiff-backed chair was brought in where he could sit and watch TV, and furniture was adjusted so Papa and his walker could squeeze through on their way to the kitchen or around the house. The only new twist was that this time I was going to be the one responsible for taking care of him.

Traditionally that job belonged to my mother, and it would have been her responsibility even if she wasn't a doctor—my childhood was enough to prove that my father was not qualified to keep another human being alive by himself. The first time my mother left town for work when I was a baby, I ended up in the emergency room after launching myself headfirst off the kitchen table. My father, who has the distinctly unhelpful tendency of fainting at the sight of blood, did an admirable job of getting me to the hospital before passing out on a spare gurney. For some reason accepting his explanation that this was a freak accident, my mom left town again six months later and I found myself in the ER again, this time after attempting to scale a bookcase which fell over on top of me, cracking the back of my head open when I rode it to the floor. These events could, perhaps, be attributed to a singularly self-destructive child, but his misdiagnosis of my chicken pox was the final nail in the coffin of his amateur medical career. After being informed that an outbreak of chicken pox had hit my first grade class and seeing me come home from school with itchy red spots all over my body, it shouldn't have taken much in the way of deductive reasoning to render a correct diagnosis. Somehow, he instead came to the conclusion that I had developed the first documented case of instantaneous full-body acne—at the age of six—and needed to take more frequent baths. Needless to say, the scalding water and vigorous scrubbing did not provide much relief.

After bringing Papa home from the hospital, my mother would be abdicating her traditional role of caretaker for the first three weeks of his recovery, as she was leading another mission group to Kenya. After she returned, several other meetings would keep her travelling. My flexible schedule and ability to work from home made me available to take care of Papa during the day while my dad was teaching at the local high school and community college, and my medical work in Kenya gave me a reasonable foundation of knowledge, at least enough that I could ask the right questions of his doctors and nurses.

Never having had anyone depend on me for anything before, I had no idea what I was getting into. Until the first day I was alone with him, I could not imagine what would be required of me. I had always depended on my parents or the college cafeteria for nourishment; often I struggled to feed myself, subsisting on a bowl of cereal in the morning and holding out until dinner, with perhaps some chips or a protein bar to keep me going. Now I would be responsible for providing three solid meals a day. The doctor recommended that Papa eat as much as he could, so I had to prepare several daily snacks as well. I was also responsible for supervising his rehabilitation exercises, ensuring he was comfortable, helping him up and down when he needed to move, and working the unfamiliar buttons on our remote—all while continuing a consulting schedule that had me working sixty hours a week.

On the first day of his recovery, I made my biggest mistake. I gave Papa a bell that he could ring if he needed anything. That bell would haunt every waking minute of the weeks ahead, and several sleeping minutes as well. He was incapable of ringing it in a way that didn't make you think his pants were on fire or that a rattlesnake had slipped in the back door, and it was only made worse by the shouted "Jesse! Jesse!" that always accompanied it. Each clanging sounded like an emergency and shot adrenaline through my body, enough that my hands were often shaking as I changed the channel or brought a fresh glass of water.

The initial days were a whirlwind. I figured out a few good snacks to make, especially apples covered in cinnamon and sugar. Cutting an apple was well within my culinary abilities and no one has ever, to my knowledge, complained about too much sugar or cinnamon on anything. When he took an afternoon nap, I would hurry down to the grocery store to stock up on food and a thick nutritional drink to get a few more calories into his healing body. I was also calling and scheduling his medical appointments, and the doorbell would ring at least once a day with a nurse or physical therapist. I would sit in on these sessions with Papa, as their advice for him was mostly directed at me. Ever the ladies' man, Papa delighted in showing the new nurses his still-healing, throat-to-sternum wound from the surgery and basking in their sympathetic cooing.

He regaled every visitor—family, friends, nurses, physical therapists—with horror stories from the hospital. "Do you know how many times they took my blood pressure? Every fifteen minutes for three days!" Or, "They tried to wake me up at three in the morning to weigh me. What were they doing?! I could have told 'em what I weigh. 185. I've been 185 for forty years! Why would they weigh me at three in the morning?" The refrains became so familiar I could mouth the words as he spoke them on the phone, and provide the supporting information that every fifteen minutes for three days would be a total of 288 blood pressure readings.

I became his "first sergeant," as he called me, cooking his meals, putting on his compression socks, making sure he took his medications and did his exercises. On the phone with his friends, he would refer to "following the sergeant's orders" and jokingly protest as I prodded him to take another lap around the house for exercise, his hospital-issued walker scraping across the hardwood of the kitchen during the commercial breaks of *The Price Is Right, Deal or No Deal,* and *Oprah.*

I knew that the confinement to a sedentary existence would rapidly start to wear on my grandfather, who had always enjoyed an active lifestyle. He was still playing tennis when he turned eighty, and I would come up to play with him during the summer. Every other Thursday he met a few of his lady friends at a local court for a game of doubles. I remember two things very distinctly about those Thursday afternoons. The first was the age of the court, completely appropriate to the age of the players. Ivy was growing all around it, cracks were starting to appear in the concrete, and it was entirely possible that the funny taste coming out of the water fountain (that no one else would drink out of) was from corroding lead pipes. The second was Papa's playing style, unique, as far as I know, in the history of the game. He was like Pete Sampras, with powerful strokes and a quick racket—if Sampras had planted himself in one position for the entire point and refused to ever move his feet. The tennis Papa could play with just his arms was incredible. He could pick up a shot that bounced right at his feet, burying his racket downward like a sword in the stone to short-hop the ball. As his doubles partner, it was my responsibility to get to any ball that didn't bounce within arm's reach of him, no matter what side it landed on. On any given point I could be charging up to get a drop shot on my side of the net, then frantically chasing down a lob to the back corner. Fortunately, this played right into my own skill set, which was hyperactivity without training or talent. Together we would hold our own against a revolving set of sixtyish, gray-haired women in little tennis outfits. Only recently I have gotten the sinking suspicion that Papa was using me as an icebreaker during these sessions, much as a cute little puppy works for other men.

Taking care of him as he recovered felt a lot like those tennis matches. He occupied the living room as I scurried around getting everything that was out of arm's reach and helping him from the bed to a chair in the morning, back to bed at night and for naps, and to the bathroom in between. We quickly fell into a rhythm. Since Papa would wake up as my dad prepared for work, they would eat breakfast together. This usually gave me a few precious hours of extra sleep in the morning, essential as I was up well past midnight every night trying to keep up with work. When I came downstairs I'd get Papa some water and help him get dressed. Before he went to sleep I would position the pee bottle next to his bed, so he wouldn't have to get up in the night, and would empty it in the morning—something that didn't exactly stoke my appetite for breakfast. Then I would coax him up for his first exercise of the day, usually a lap around the house. Stuck in his chair, he found a schedule as well, revolving mostly around television reruns. The time between *The Price Is Right* and *Deal or No Deal* was filled with a nap and lunch, usually soup and crackers (also within my culinary wheelhouse).

Despite the challenges, the first few days of his recovery were exciting. I kept track of his progress with a chart on the fridge, tallying each completed lap. He was improving rapidly, going from two to four to eight laps around the house in the first three days. The revolving door of medical professionals was still new and interesting, and we entertained hopes of being back out on the golf course together in a couple of months. I was providing constant encouragement, hoping to keep his spirits up during his confinement. I even did the math and determined that if he continued improving at the current rate he could be finishing a house-lap marathon in less than three weeks.

I knew something was wrong on the third day, when I didn't hear any movement when I came down the stairs in the morning. The first two days Papa had been up and watching the morning news, waiting for me in his chair. This morning the silence was heavy. He was still on the bed, on his back, mouth open and unmoving. I couldn't see any rise or fall of his chest. Relief washed over me when I heard a weak breath trickling out of his throat.

He slept for more than fourteen hours. When he finally stirred I helped him out of bed, calling him Sleeping Beauty and making light of the situation, but it was clear that something had changed. Visibly exhausted—he would sleep for another three hours that afternoon, and spent less than four hours out of bed that day—it was the beginning of a terrifying downward spiral.

That day his recovery stopped and reversed itself, like we were playing the tape backwards. I didn't know what I could do to break the cycle—should I try to get him up and restore a normal schedule, or just let him sleep? In the end, I decided to let him listen to his body, sleeping as much as he could, but he never seemed to catch up with his exhaustion.

As the days passed he began coughing more, frightening jags that left him gasping for air, eyes wide. The hospital had given Papa a red, heart-shaped pillow that he was supposed to clutch to his chest when he coughed, preventing his wound from breaking open under the strain. It was never close enough for him to reach, so at the first hint of a cough I would run in, finding the pillow and getting it into his arms. The coughs emanated from deep in his chest with a horrifying wetness to them, but his lungs weren't strong enough to cough up anything. I was watching him drown.

His legs began to swell, ballooning with the same fluid that was filling his lungs; his heart wasn't strong enough to pump it away. The bones in his feet and ankles disappeared entirely, making it much more difficult for him to walk. Every step was treacherous. He often needed several tries to get out of his chair, each accompanied by a huge groan of exertion. I would follow behind him in the narrow hallway with my hand on his lower back, supporting him on the way to the bathroom. His faltering steps were accompanied by a rhythmic noise under his breath and I couldn't help but laugh, despite the situation, when I realized he was muttering "shit, shit, shit" in time with his footsteps. You don't expect to hear four-letter words coming out of people with gray hair, and it might have been the first swear word ever uttered in my parents' house. The first time we reached the bathroom door together there was an awkward pause. I asked if he was going to be all right in there, and was relieved when he said yes. Anxiously I waited outside, door slightly ajar, fearing that my reluctance to help him in the bathroom would result in a fall. In the confines of the small guest bathroom, between the granite counters, toilet, and bathtub, there weren't many forgiving surfaces where he could land.

To combat the swelling in his feet, the doctor had sent Papa home with a pair of compression socks. They fit as tightly as possible, with the goal of forcing the fluid out of his lower legs. Every night I would take them off, straining to pull the fabric over his heel and off his foot. Getting them back on in the morning was much, much worse. I needed both hands to hold the sock open, and in his weakened state Papa couldn't provide any resistance. Resting his leg awkwardly across my knee, I would pin it between my arm and chest to keep it steady, covering his foot with the sock as quickly as possible to hide his long, yellowed toenails from sight. Yanking and tugging the sock up his leg, I smoothed out any wrinkles. Trapping his leg between my chest and arm reminded me of the way he would remove slivers when I was a kid, restraining my arm and dexterously removing the offending piece of wood with a knife, a technique he had perfected on the junior employees in his woodshop.

With his legs heavily swollen, the task became even more arduous. After about a week, I felt moisture against the backs of my hands—the swelling had strained his legs to the breaking point and was beginning to weep out of invisible cracks in the skin. We began leaving the socks on through the night, trying to reduce the swelling. I rubbed his legs with lotion every time the socks came off, but his skin split further, angry cracks canvassing his lower legs. Nothing was worse than hearing his sharp intake of breath when I had to drag those socks over his open sores, though he never uttered a word of complaint. I hated those damn socks.

Although the bones had disappeared in his feet, they were becoming more and more pronounced in his face. His gray complexion and weight loss gave Papa a skeletal visage. The nurses provided by the home health service weren't any help. We never got the same one twice, and I wouldn't be surprised if they all had gotten degrees from the same Turkish correspondence course. Their only suggestions were food, water, and rest—as if I thought that starving him and waking him up every two hours was a better option. No one could tell me what to do about his coughing, the sores on his legs, or the fluid building up in his lungs. Because they were always new, they couldn't see what I saw—my grandfather was slowly wasting away. Unable to breathe deeply, he was constantly short of breath. The optimism after his release from the hospital faded into fear and frustration at his continued infirmity as the days dragged on.

CHAPTER 6

Life in the Camp

It is most strongly felt that the camp commander with his staff have no interest whatsoever in the welfare of the prisoners of war.

—SWISS DELEGATE, REPORT FROM STALAG IXB, 1945

Feb 6: Got strafed, two killed in barracks, five injured, plenty close. Allies shot down plane. One of the two killed was next to me—missed me by one foot.

—ROBERT COZEAN, PRISON DIARY, 1945

THE HIGH-PITCHED DRONE OF ENGINES BROKE THE QUIET OF camp life, foreshadowing the arrival of several American planes pursuing a Luftwaffe fighter. Those prisoners who were outside looked up to watch, enthralled at the life-or-death chase in the sky above and elated at their first glimpse of the American war machine, bringing hope for liberation. For the POWs, the whirling dogfight was a welcome break from the monotony of daily life in Stalag IXB, at least for the few men braving the cold February air outside the scant protection of the broken-down barracks. The men were eager to see their first glimpse of an American victory—for most of the men, the Battle of the Bulge had been their first, and only, fighting experience in the war. As they watched, the German plane flew over the camp, hoping the trailing attackers would break off pursuit. But the location of the prisoners was unknown to the pilots, and the American gunners began to fire hundreds of .50-caliber rounds down at the German plane, and the barracks below.

Holes the size of a man's fist appeared in the roof, the bullets striking before the prisoners inside could even hear the guns firing. Two men were instantly killed, one nearly cut in half by the machine gun fire. Another man, lying in the top bunk, saw a bullet cut a line through his jacket without even grazing him, instantly earning him the nickname Mr. Lucky. Then the planes were gone, the German pilot shot down in flames. The guards soon appeared, ordering the prisoners to mop up the blood of their friends. That day, February 6, marked the longest entry in my grandfather's journal. "Got strafed, two killed in barracks, five injured, plenty close. Allies shot down plane. One of the two killed was next to me—missed me by one foot."

The next day the prisoners used white lime powder to spell out "POW" on the grass, alerting American planes of their presence. A noticeable pall fell over the camp, as the attack brought home the danger of their situation. Papa knew it could have just as easily been his blood being mopped off the floor.

When my grandfather arrived at Stalag IXB, a steel helmet was passed around to relieve the captured soldiers of their money, watches, jewelry, cigarettes, and any other valuables that might burden them during their stay. The U.S. Army had just paid the soldiers before shipping them to the front lines of the war, so the German guards received quite a bonus, 1,930 Belgian francs, courtesy of Papa. The prisoners were also questioned about their military experience and what they had done for a living before the war. My grandfather told the Germans he was a farmer, hoping they might ask him to work in the fields of the camp.

Although Papa filled out a Red Cross form on January 1, six days after his admittance to the camp, Kitty wouldn't learn he was a prisoner of war, and not dead, until March 6—all she knew was that her husband was missing in action.

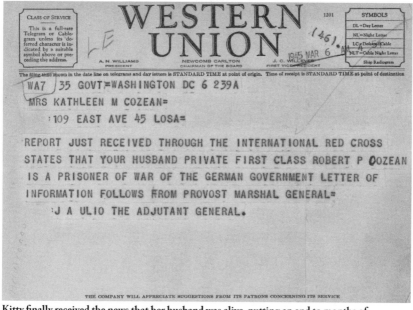

Kitty finally received the news that her husband was alive, putting an end to months of uncertainty.

On January 5, he was permitted to write a letter home, which arrived several months later. It is a window into his time at the camp, exhibiting his unflagging optimism, the gnawing hunger

Good News for Kathleen

Sometimes these wartime telegram bring good news!

Such a one came March 6th to Kathleen Cozean, secretary in Product Engineering. It was from the International Red Cross, and said that her husband, Robert, declared missing in a War Department wire on Jan. 12th, was in a German prison camp at Bad Orb, some 80 miles from Coblenz.

Pfc. Robert Cozean

Robert and Kathleen have been married three years. He was a graduate of Lincoln High in 1938. In March, 1944, he entered the service, was assigned to the infantry and received most of his training at Camp Fannin, Tex. He reached England in October, and was soon shipped to France. Kathleen's last letter from him was dated Dec. 13th. He was taken prisoner three days later, when the great German counter-offensive was launched on the 16th.

Kathleen has been at Cannon's for a little more than three years.

The article from the local paper, upon learning that Papa had survived the attack and been taken prisoner.

The standard Red Cross envelope that contained Papa's first letter to Kitty from the camp. The instructions are in German, the language of the country, and French, the language used by the International Red Cross in Geneva. On the top left is the stamp of Stalag IXB.

that would be his constant companion in camp, and the longing for the wife he had left behind.

January 5, 1945
Dearest Kitty:
I hope you know by now that I am a prisoner of war and am not missing in action and I wasn't wounded so I am all right. So don't worry about me. Send me a package. Contact the Red Cross and find out how you go about sending it to me so I will be sure of getting it. Send me some cheese Kraft 2 lbs of it, jelly, a jar, graham crackers, sugar and some candy. Send as much as you can and as often as you can as I didn't receive any packages you sent due to being captured.

Sweets, remember I love you more each day and I am always thinking about you each moment of the day. As I have plenty of time to think now. Last letter I received was dated Dec 3 so after that I won't get any. A million kisses.
Lots of Love—Bob

Papa told me that although he was also able to send a few Red Cross postcards home while in the camp, none of her responses were ever delivered. His correspondence with her prompted a small article in the local paper:

Robert P. Cozean
Three cards and a letter have been received from Private First Class Robert P. Cozean, a 24-year old local youth who has been a prisoner of war in Germany since December 16, when he was captured in the German counter-offensive into Belgium.

Husband of Mrs. Kathleen Cozean, of 109 East Avenue 45, he entered the army in March, 1944, was trained in the infantry at Camp Fannin, Texas, and was sent overseas last October, going first to England, later to France, and then into Germany.

Private Cozean is a graduate of Lincoln high school and Frank Wiggins trade school, and is the son of Mr. and Mrs. W.B. Cozean, of 2316½ Workman Street.

Looking back, Papa's account of his time in the camp was weeks of boredom on end, suddenly shattered by brief moments of terror and constantly shadowed by filth, disease, hunger, and cold. The prisoners were assigned one work detail per week, the rest of their time spent in the barracks or outside for brief stretches on sunny days, where they spoke about food and avoided the pressing subjects of their capture or chances for survival. No conversations centered on escape, at least none that Papa heard. When they first arrived at the camp, the Germans told them that for every man who tried to escape, they would kill twenty more. And, as my grandfather put it, "even if we walked out of there, there was nowhere to go." The prisoners were hundreds of miles from where they had been captured, what they saw as an impossible distance to cover in their emaciated state without food or clothing. With the twin threats of repercussions for their friends and the harsh reality of a German winter arrayed against them, thoughts of escape were quickly abandoned.

During the short winter days the men would stay inside the barracks as much as possible, trying to conserve what warmth they could. They were too weak from hunger to be very active, though they were allowed the run of the camp during the day. Beyond trips to use the outdoor latrines, the prisoners were required to attend the daily roll call, often in freezing weather, where the German guards counted and recounted the men, seemingly unsure of the number of prisoners they needed to confirm. Sometimes a prisoner would be too weak to make it out of the barracks. My grandfather remembers men being counted in the front ranks of the line and waiting for the German guard to pass, then ducking low and sneaking to the back to be counted again to cover for a sick companion. When night fell the German guards would walk through the camp, closing and padlocking the doors to the barracks. The POWs would remain locked in until the morning.

Work details were widely varied: firewood detail, burial detail, the coveted potato wagon. Each afternoon members of the firewood detail would carry huge armfuls of dead wood in from the forest surrounding the camp. Only one armful per man was allowed, so the men would stagger in with as much as they could carry in their weakened state to warm the barracks. The burial detail dug the graves and disposed of the bodies of their comrades. Those on the potato wagon were responsible for transporting food into the camp and unloading it in the kitchen. They would hastily fill their pockets with potatoes for themselves and their friends, or at least be able to surreptitiously nibble on their cargo as they worked. Papa was assigned to the dreaded "honey wagon" throughout his time in camp—shoveling out the latrine and moving the contents outside the camp grounds. He told me, "the only thing worse than being half-starved and shoveling shit out of a cesspool is not being able to shower afterward."

As weeks of captivity turned into months, clothes began to fray and fall apart and lice became the only well-fed group in the camp. My grandfather could still remember feeling them constantly skittering over his skin, running up and down his legs at night and feeling them under his belt buckle during the day. The only relief was on rare sunny days, when he could go outside, open up his waistband, and watch the little bastards die in the sunlight. Although under the terms of the Geneva Convention it was the duty of the Germans to provide clothing for the men they had imprisoned, they instead had confiscated anything that the prisoners weren't wearing, leaving them with only their thin Army uniforms for their entire captivity.

Each barracks building housed between three hundred and five hundred men each, with a single washroom located in the middle of the building. The washroom, if it could be called that—it would be suicidal to wash with cold water in the midst of a harsh northern Germany winter—contained only a single cold water tap and one latrine. As soon as the men were introduced to the watery soup they became sick. At night the men would be stumbling over each other as they ran to the hole in the ground, which soon became foul. No toilet paper was provided, so the prisoners used what they could, usually leaves or the dirty straw that covered the floor. Paper was too precious to use. Even the outside latrines only contained forty stalls, completely insufficient for the number of men detained in the camp.

The prisoners, at least the lucky ones, slept two or three to a bed on bare wooden slats, waking with bruises on their hips and shoulders from the hard surface. Bunk beds filled the barracks, stacked three high, meaning the men in the bottom bunk could have as many as six men above them. The unlucky men, nearly fifteen hundred of them, did not have bunks at all and curled up on the floor, wherever they could find room. The wind whipped through the broken windows and poor wooden construction of the barracks, and the roofs leaked everywhere. Even if more beds had been provided, the men would have still had to sleep together in order to survive the freezing nights—the Germans only provided half of a horse blanket for each man, probably surplus from World War I.

The prisoners survived the nights by pairing up and sleeping back to back, directly on the wooden slats of the bunk beds that filled the barracks. My grandfather bunked with a man named Charles, from Tennessee, who became a life-long friend.

Charles had been a salesman for the Ford Motor Company, selling new models at a dealership in Tennessee, before he was drafted and sent to fight Hitler. Like my grandfather, who was trained as a weapons mechanic, Charles was given a specialty. He served as a secretary as well as a soldier, filling out the forms and taking care of the bureaucratic details that keep the Army running smoothly. They met in England, while waiting to be transported across the Channel to France and the front lines. My grandfather saw him standing around and asked if he wanted to head into town. At thirty-three years old, Charles was ten years older than Papa, an elder statesman among the prisoners, who were mostly in their teens or early twenties.

The two men watched out for each other in the camp. Papa put it simply. "To survive in the prison camp you had to have a buddy to help you, and you helped him." It was vital to have someone to encourage you when you were overwhelmed or despairing, to pull you out of the darkness and make you focus on the hope of freedom. Charles and Papa did this for each other on a daily basis, talking about the food they would eat and the dreams they would fulfill when they were liberated.

After the war they kept in touch by phone, and my grandfather and his family would often pack up the car and take a driving vacation out to see Charles and his family in Memphis. When my grandfather was recovering from his heart surgery, he received a call from a woman named Dorothy. After they spoke I asked him who Dorothy was, as I had talked to most of his friends over the past few days and didn't recognize the name. Dorothy was Charles's wife, a former Ford Motor Company model. Charles had died nearly fifteen years before, but she and my grandfather still spoke by phone about once a month.

The cruelty in the camp was deliberate, orchestrated, and premeditated, but I was surprised to hear there was relatively little malicious interaction between the guards and prisoners. The language barrier prevented much communication between the two groups and, as escape was extremely improbable, an uneasy peace existed between them. A POW could still draw a rifle butt across the back or head if he didn't move quickly enough, but most learned to avoid provoking their captors. Occasionally the prisoners would even tease a German by saying, "General Patton is coming." Another mischievous German-speaking prisoner taught a guard, eager to learn some English to impress his superiors, the translation of *Achtung* (Attention!). For the next several weeks, the prisoners were called to attention at morning roll call by the ambitious German guard bellowing "Bullshit!"

At times German guards even demonstrated great kindness and empathy toward the prisoners. U.S. Army intelligence reports specifically name one guard at the camp, Gefreiter Weiss, who risked his life to inform the prisoners about the progress of the war and the location of advancing American troops.

At the same time, conditions in Stalag IXB were deliberately inhumane for the captured soldiers. The men were slowly starving to death as pneumonia, dysentery, influenza, grippe, and bronchitis ravaged the camp, taking advantage of the crowded barracks and the weakened condition of the men. To make matters worse, the Germans had appropriated the Red Cross medical supplies meant for the prisoners, citing "transportation breakdowns." Upon visiting the camp in March, three months after the men had been captured, a Red Cross representative reported:

The situation here may be considered very serious. The personal impression which one gets from an inspection tour

*of these camps cannot be described. One discovers distress
and famine in their most terrible forms . . . These prisoners,
in rags, covered with filth and infested with vermin, live
crowded together in barracks, when they do not lie under
tents, squeezed together on the ground on a thin pallet of
dirty straw or 2 or 3 per cot, or on benches and tables. Some
of them are scarcely able to get up, or else they fall in a
swoon as they did when they tried to get up when the Representative was passing through. They do not move, even
at meal time, when they are presented with their inadequate German rations.*

Another delegate from the neutral country of Switzerland
also visited the camp. After inspecting Stalag IXB, he reported:

*It is most strongly felt that the camp commander with his
staff have no interest whatsoever in the welfare of the prisoners of war. This is clearly shown by the fact that although he
made many promises on our last visit, he has not even tried to
ameliorate conditions and is apt to blame the Allies for these
conditions.*

In the German prison camps there was a definitive hierarchy
among the POWs. The Poles, Serbs, and Russians were treated
far worse than their Western European or American counter-
parts. In general, the war on the Eastern Front was much more
brutal than the fighting in the west. More men fought and died
on the Eastern Front than in any other theater of any other war
in history, and atrocities were regularly committed by both the
Soviets and Germans. Upon occupying Soviet territory, the

German SS rounded up as many Jews as they could find and shot them—34,777 at once in a massacre at Babi Yar. After three years of German occupation, between one and two million Soviet Jews were murdered in their homes, villages, and in concentration camps. Many other civilians shared the same fate, or were starved to death when the German Army seized their food. A total of twenty-seven million Soviets were killed during World War II, more than half of them civilians. The Soviet Union was just as guilty, murdering captured Polish prisoners on the direct order of Joseph Stalin in 1940. Of the ninety-one thousand German soldiers captured by the USSR at the Battle of Stalingrad, fewer than five thousand survived.

The harsh conditions for Russian POWs in the camps caused huge casualties. During the entire course of the war, Germany and her allies captured 5.7 million Soviets. About a million of these prisoners were released by the Germans, another half million escaped or were rescued during the war, and 930,000 were found alive in prison camps after the invasion of Germany. All others, more than three million, died in captivity. More than half of all Soviet prisoners taken did not survive to be released. Even worse, after all they endured the prisoners were viewed as traitors by the Soviet leadership because they had surrendered instead of fighting to the death. Upon returning to their homeland, many were imprisoned by their own government, and the rest were disgraced and unable to find work.

The persecution of the Eastern European POWs was a systematic policy that was instituted from German leadership. The German POW regulations stated: "223. Re: Shooting and severe wounding of prisoners of war and civilian internees (except Poles, Serbs, and Soviet Russians). An inquiry by a court officer or any other qualified officer is to be initiated in each case of fatal shooting or wounding of a British, French, Belgian, or American prisoner of war or civilian internee." No investigation was required into the death of a Polish, Serbian, or Soviet prisoner, and they could be shot at the slightest provocation. Their deaths went unreported.

This discrepancy was obvious at Stalag IXB. The Russians were walled off in their own part of the camp, and conditions for them were even worse than for my grandfather. A graveyard outside the camp is still visible, sixty-five years later. It holds the bodies of the 1,430 Russian prisoners who died in captivity at Stalag IXB of hunger, cold, and illness. Only 356 of their names were known.

Even within the American ranks treatment could vary greatly. According to the Geneva Convention, officers were exempted from being put to work by their captors, while enlisted men could be pressed into labor as long as it wasn't directly aiding the war effort. Officers were detached from the men of their command and imprisoned in separate facilities.

In the POW camps, as in the rest of Nazi-occupied Europe, Jews were identified and systematically discriminated against. The German POW Regulations regarding the marking of Jews are clear: "The Jews in Germany are specially marked with a star, as a measure of the German government to identify them in the streets, stores, etc. Jewish prisoners of war are not marked with a star, yet they have to be kept apart from the other prisoners of war as far as possible." Jews were often separated into their own camps or barracks, and invariably they were worked harder, at more dangerous tasks, than the other POWs. Older prisoners saved many incoming POWs from this fate by warning them against disclosing their heritage. The attitude of Germany as a whole toward the Jews can be seen in their POW regulations:

111. Re: Prisoners of War as blood donors.

For reasons of race hygiene, prisoners of war are not acceptable as blood donors for members of the German community, since the possibility of a prisoner of war of Jewish origin being used as a donor cannot be excluded with certainty.

Stalag IXB, infamous for being one of the worst German prison camps, was also the only place where American POWs were sent to a concentration camp—including as many Jews as the Germans could identify. The guards began by segregating the Jewish POWs into their own barracks. This was accomplished in several ways by the camp authorities. American dog tags, the ID tags that soldiers are required to wear at all times, carried a mark for religious preference, so that the appropriate pastor, priest, or rabbi could be provided for a dying man. Troops would either have a P (Protestant), C (Catholic), or H (Hebrew) stamped on their tags. This made it easy for the commandant to identify many Jewish prisoners. Captured Jewish soldiers were faced with a difficult choice—keep their dog tags when they surrendered and be identified as *Juden,* or throw them away and risk being shot as a spy.

Guards also distributed a questionnaire to the prisoners, regarding their home address, employment, parents' names, and religion. The Geneva Convention only requires a captured soldier to provide name, rank, and serial number, but this form was used to segregate anyone who marked "Jewish" from the rest of the men.

Finally, the camp authorities pressured the POWs to betray their comrades. The prisoners had elected a leader, known as "The Man of Confidence," to be responsible for communication with the German guards. When Private Kasten, the Man of Confidence, refused the order to name all the Jews in the American barracks, two German officers threw him down a flight of stairs. He survived, and told each barracks leader to warn their men against identifying themselves as Jewish if they hadn't already been discovered. The next day the commandant assembled all the POWs and demanded that the Jews step forward. When no one moved, the commandant himself borrowed a rifle from a guard and clubbed Kasten to the ground with it. Several German guards then walked through the ranks of men, identifying those they thought looked Jewish. My grandfather's blue eyes certainly helped him avoid being selected. Some men betrayed their Jewish comrades, forcing them to step forward, but most of the camp worked to conceal their presence.

Those who were selected were rounded up and put in Forty and Eights, bound for the concentration camp at Berga. Along with those suspected of being Jews, the Germans also sent those they considered troublemakers. Private Kasten was responsible for counting the prisoners as they entered the boxcar. For his refusal to single out the Jews in the camp, Kasten was given the last spot on his own roster. A total of 350 men, 77 of Jewish heritage, were shipped out.

Those who survived the war reported that after five days in the boxcar, they were put to work at Berga, digging tunnels 150 feet below ground to store ammunition. It was difficult and extraordinarily dangerous work, especially for men who were severely malnourished. They worked alongside the skeletal Jews of the concentration camp who had managed to survive, witnessing public hangings and beatings every day. More than two dozen of the POWs from Papa's camp would die in the tunnels. When the American army began drawing near at the end of the war, the survivors were taken on an eighteen-day death march. They slept in barns, abandoned castles, and out in fields. Men who died were buried by the side of the road, before the guards forced the rest of the men to keep moving. Forty-eight men who began that march died with rescue only a few miles away. All told, more than a quarter of the men who were shipped out of Stalag IXB would not live to see the end of the war.

As Americans, rightfully proud of the sacrifices we made to defeat Hitler's twisted vision of a master race, we generally don't appreciate the greatest irony of World War II—we went to war with the most infamous racist in modern history with a segregated army. Black troops were placed in separate units, typically commanded by white officers. No black officer would be allowed to command a white man. African-American servicemen generally worked as laborers, rather than as front-line troops. Prior to World War II, the Army Air Corps dealt with the expense of having to provide separate housing and facilities for blacks by not allowing any to join. During the war at military bases in the South, restaurants would turn away black American soldiers while serving captured Nazi POWs.

However, over the course of the war, segregation began to fall apart out of necessity. At the Battle of the Bulge, where my grandfather was captured, the U.S. Army was being pushed backwards by the desperate final offensive by Germany. Overwhelmingly outnumbered, the Army asked for any black servicemen who wished to volunteer to fight. More than forty-five hundred did so and were quickly formed into provisional platoons and sent into the battle—for the first time fighting alongside their white countrymen. After the war the official policy of segregation in the armed forces was finally ended, although it took several years to completely integrate the military.

Also, while the Third Reich was building concentration camps throughout Europe, the United States government systematically rounded up 110,000 Japanese-Americans, mostly citizens of our country. Charged with no crime, they were imprisoned in "War Relocation Camps." Some German-Americans and Italian-Americans were also detained in camps run, ironically enough, by the Justice Department. It took until 1988, two years after I was born, for the United States government to finally apologize for these actions, admitting that the discrimination toward these American citizens was "race prejudice, war hysteria, and a failure of political leadership."

— ~ —

However mundane daily life in the camp seemed, the men could not relax knowing that their lives were entirely in the hands of their captors. The monotony of camp life and the coexistence of German guards and American prisoners were shattered by several major incidents throughout my grandfather's imprisonment. One winter morning during roll call, with heavily falling snow blanketing the camp, the Germans became agitated, pacing and yelling. The prisoners who could understand German passed the word—an escape. The German promise to execute twenty men if one escaped was etched in Papa's mind. Holding the men at gunpoint, the German guards demanded to know the location of the missing prisoner, threatening to begin shooting if no one came forward with knowledge of the escape. Dressed in the tattered remains of their uniforms and holding perfectly still to avoid the wrath of the enraged guards, the cold began to seep into their bones. No one confessed any knowledge of the escape, and the men shivered in the snow, sure they would be cut down by bullets or the harsh winter, unable or unwilling to provide answers. The Germans finally caught the "escaped" prisoner—lying dead in his bunk, weakened by starvation and killed by the cold.

The chaplain was probably the busiest of the men, planning weekly Protestant and Catholic services as well as two or three funerals a week during Papa's four months of imprisonment. As the men became weaker and more susceptible to the cold and disease, the death toll continued to rise and their captors became efficient at putting bodies into the ground, using a specially built casket. From the outside it looked like a normal coffin— the deceased was placed inside, it could be carried and viewed at the funeral—but it featured a hidden trapdoor at the back. When the service was concluded, the prisoners on burial detail would carry the casket away. Pulling a lever allowed the body to tumble out into a pit, where they would cover the corpse in lime to decompose the body and shovel a few spadefuls of dirt on top. The casket was then ready for its next occupant. Not quite what one would expect from the German POW Regulations, which stated, "As a matter of principle, every honorable fallen enemy is to be buried with military honors." The men killed by their own planes joined the casualties of starvation and disease in the mass grave as the casket was used again.

CHAPTER 7

The Fall

BEING CARED FOR WAS DIFFICULT FOR PAPA; IT RAN COUNTER to everything he stood for. He had started taking care of himself as soon as he graduated from high school and remained fiercely independent in his old age. In my insecure moments I wondered what Papa thought of me—I had moved back into my parents' house at the age of twenty and stayed for another two years (and counting), I work at a computer instead of a job site, and when a tire bursts I reach for my cell phone instead of a tire jack, letting AAA do the heavy lifting. I can intelligently discuss what happens to subatomic particles moving at nearly the speed of light, but if my car doesn't work and the gas gauge doesn't read E, I'm in trouble. With Papa now living in the same house and seeing my daily life, I was worried that his opinion of me might be steadily dropping.

For sixty-five years, Papa had been taking care of himself and others—supporting his wife throughout their marriage, helping Charles survive Stalag IXB, caring for his kids and later his grandkids. Shortly after each grandchild was born, he set aside a college savings account for each of us that would give us $5,000 when we finished school. Even though that money made only a small dent in my massive student loan debt, that gesture was an unspoken but reassuring sign of his approval.

One of my earliest memories of Papa was the last time we went backpacking together. He, my father, and a scrawny ten-year-old loaded up packs and set off into the wilderness—perhaps hoping to get some family bonding time, or at least finally nail down all the potential driving routes between our homes. I was struck with a vicious case of altitude sickness. For the first two days my head was pounding, and I was so constantly nauseated that everything I sent down came back up again. I can still remember my father being strangely unperturbed that his only son was tossing his cookies by the side of the trail. Only Papa seemed to worry that I hadn't digested anything in forty-eight hours. At least, since we were hiking, my dad couldn't try to cure me with a bath. On the third night we set up camp early, and they agreed if I wasn't better in the morning we would cancel the rest of the trip and head back to civilization.

As soon as my throbbing head hit the inflatable pillow, I was out. Blissfully unconscious for the next ten hours, I woke up pain free and ravenous. Papa and my dad were outside the tent, cooking on our small gas stove. Emerging from the cocoon of the tent, I began shoveling pancakes into my mouth as fast as they could flip them, with only a slight pause to let them cool and douse them with syrup, no utensils necessary. The batter made twenty-four pancakes—Papa and my dad managed to snag four between them as I wolfed down the rest.

As difficult as it was for me to take responsibility for someone else, it must have been just as hard for Papa to accept being taken care of. It had been two weeks since he came home from the surgery, and Papa continued to decline. His heart wasn't able to circulate enough blood, leaving his skin a dull gray. The only thing that brought color to his face were his deep, racking coughing fits. His legs continued to swell, becoming even more painful. Even worse, fluid continued collecting in his lungs, making every breath an effort. Sitting across from him at the kitchen table, I could hear the sickening gurgle that accompanied each exhalation. Emanating from deep in his throat, it sounded like a noisy dishwasher as water pours through it.

Because he was struggling to breathe, we purchased a gadget used to measure the amount of oxygen in his blood. A normal person, I learned, typically has a blood-oxygen reading between 95 and 100, which can safely drop to around 90 after heavy exercise. So on the first day of basketball conditioning, when I was cursing the coach and his whistle, struggling to catch my breath, and feeling like my heart was about to explode out of my chest, my oxygen level would have been about 90. The first time I measured Papa, after he had been sitting for several hours, the meter read 84. Over the next few days I measured every hour, marking the measurements on a chart. When he was sitting it would be around 85, and would plummet to below 80 as soon as he stood up to move to the kitchen table or bathroom.

All thoughts of physical therapy or exercise to help him recover were gone—he was working hard enough to just catch his breath or make it to the bathroom. I was watching him slowly suffocate as fluid filled his lungs. My sole mission was keeping him alive until the follow-up appointment with his doctor at the end of the week.

Waiting until he was in the bathroom or napping to avoid letting him know how grave his condition seemed, I called the surgeon's office daily, alternating between demanding and pleading that they move up his post-op appointment. The receptionist, whose only qualification seemed to be her cultish devotion to preserving the surgeon's tee time, steadfastly insisted moving up the appointment was impossible.

With four days to go before his appointment Papa was getting less lucid, waking up confused in the morning and from his naps. Thinking he was in his own bedroom, he would reach for his glasses to where his nightstand should be and nearly topple out of bed. It would take several minutes before he remembered where he was. He was also much more unsteady on his feet, and I watched him as carefully as I could, concerned that he would suffer a fall on his way to the bathroom or kitchen.

Despite everything, I never heard my grandfather complain. When I came in to check on him, I would refill his water and add some ice, but he had fewer and fewer requests. The only thing worse than the constant clanging of the bell was its conspicuous absence. I would look up from my work and realize several hours had passed without hearing from him. I would rush into the living room, finding him semiconscious in the chair.

Papa was so constantly exhausted that even discussing his wartime experiences didn't interest him. I had begun typing up the notes from our first interview, hoping to eventually present Papa with a full copy of his story. I had even used the time to scan and include many of the pictures, telegrams, and other documents in Papa's war binder. As I was writing I would have questions about the order of events or small details that I would bring to him. His eyes didn't light up like they used to when I asked—his answers were generally confined to just a grunt or nod, and sometimes he didn't answer at all. Eventually I stopped asking, waiting for him to bring it up again.

Trying to make sure he got enough rest, I made a rule I would repeat over and over again, "No sleeping in the chair." If he was exhausted enough to sleep, I wanted him comfortable and safe in bed instead of nodding off while sitting up. I had to help him to bed now, supporting his weight as he shuffled across the three feet from the chair back to bed. I would sit him down on the mattress, then lean him back and lift his legs to lay him flat. He slept exclusively on his back, and even when asleep I couldn't be sure he was safe. I would come in a few minutes later to find one leg dangling off the bed and his head tilted back at an unnatural angle. Papa was so tired he wouldn't stir, even when about to tumble to the floor. Gently lifting his legs, I would try to scoot them toward the middle of bed and safety. I could even raise his head and slip the pillow back underneath without waking him. Because he needed constant supervision, I moved my work onto the kitchen table.

He was spending more time in his confused, semiconscious state. The lack of oxygen flowing to his brain quickly turned his confusion into hallucinations and particularly vivid dreams. Almost fortunately for me, he began chattering away in his sleep—it was my only assurance he wasn't dead. Sometimes it would be just noise, his mouth opening and closing as he spewed nonsensical syllables. Other times he would be lying in bed, talking on a phone that existed only in his mind. I stopped to listen, wondering if I would be eavesdropping on his innermost thoughts. I had to laugh when I realized all I was hearing was a report on the state of the Dodgers or driving directions to the store.

I am ashamed to realize, after only a few weeks, how frustrated I was by all the inconveniences that this caretaking had imposed. No doubt being sleep-deprived had something to do with it, but the grueling schedule was starting to take its toll. I was still trying to work full-time, but each day was constantly interrupted by calls for more water, to let in a nurse, or to help him to the bathroom. I tried, unsuccessfully, to catch up while he was napping or late at night. I hadn't been to the gym or out with friends since Papa arrived, and had no outlet to blow off steam. My office had migrated to the kitchen table, surrounded by old newspapers and encrusted with dropped Wheaties flakes. I couldn't even watch a movie to relax—Papa would have slept through a tornado, but his sleeping babble would drown out the sound. Incredibly, the only thing he couldn't sleep through was having the television turned off. The best I could do was slowly lower the volume throughout his afternoon nap.

The thought struck me that this must be what having a kid is like—without the nine months of warning—though I have no way of knowing if that comparison is accurate or not. My life revolved around his schedule, with everything I used to think was important subjugated to his needs. I was up when he was up, cooking when he was hungry, and quiet when he was sleeping. I used to have music playing as I worked, but couldn't risk that something would happen to him without me being able to hear it. And whatever he wanted to watch was on the television. I think I would have preferred *Sesame Street* to another afternoon of *Oprah*. I tried to suppress my little flashes of irritation, feeling incredibly guilty about harboring uncharitable thoughts as he was fighting for breath.

The worst of these flashes occurred one morning after I had spent most of the night, until 4:00 a.m., catching up on a big work project. I had left out a bowl, spoon, and his Wheaties for the morning, so that I could sleep in for a few precious hours. At 7:15 I woke to the sound of the urgently clanging bell. I am not at my best in the morning, and certainly not after less than three hours of rest, but I threw on a pair of shorts and bolted downstairs, wondering what kind of medical emergency I was going to have to deal with. "Jesse! Jesse!" he yelled. Taking the stairs three at a time, I was surprised to find him on his feet—clearly not in cardiac or respiratory failure—swinging the damn dinner bell like a modern-day Quasimodo, down to the hunchbacked posture as he steadied himself with a free hand on his walker.

The emergency that caused the racket and interrupted my sleep was that the television wasn't working and he needed me to get the morning news on for him. Evidently it was difficult for him to nap in his chair without a droning news anchor. I couldn't go back to sleep—with the way I had woken up, running a marathon was more likely. My thoughts were less than charitable at that point as I stabbed the buttons of the remote control vindictively. Needless to say, the prospect of getting him back home was the light at the end of the tunnel, both because I loved Papa and knew how important his independence was to him and because it removed the temptation to strangle him.

There was still a brand new nurse coming by each day, each leaving more and more concerned. I persuaded one of them to order an oxygen concentrator for him after showing her the measurements that I had recorded over the last few days. She acquiesced, and it arrived the next day. The device is like a vacuum cleaner with its wires reversed, sucking in the ambient air and pumping oxygen-enriched air through little tubes. The thin tubes wrapped around his head, around his ears, and over his upper lip to deliver the oxygen directly to his nostrils. Papa was so weak that when he raised his arms over his head they trembled uncontrollably, making it impossible to position the tubing, so I would do it for him, hands brushing the side of his face and the mustache he was now growing.

The nurse—clearly not knowing anything more than I did about the oxygen concentrator, as I had to all but beg for it—recommended we only use it an hour or so each day, to help him catch his breath after exertion. I thoughtfully nodded at her advice at the appropriate times, thanked her profusely for ordering the machine, and promptly ignored her instructions. I'm not a doctor, but even I know that oxygen deprivation isn't the preferred treatment for many conditions. Even with the oxygen concentrator, his blood oxygen level peaked at 88, still in the dangerous range. Even as he was receiving pure oxygen, Papa continued losing his grasp on reality.

I remember seeing my grandfather hallucinate before, after his knee replacement, but that was in the comforting confines of a hospital, with trained medical personnel on call. At that time, without the responsibility for caring for him and knowing it was only a temporary reaction to his medication, it was actually pretty funny. After getting over the initial shock, I enjoyed his detailed descriptions of what his mind was producing. He described seeing a parade of exotic animals traipsing through the hospital room. From the sound of it, his mind was producing a fusion of an African safari and the dancing elephants of *Fantasia*. Sitting with him during those long afternoons, I discovered that the one thing that could bring him back to the present were questions about woodworking. My repeated questions about the proper way to hang a door and where to place the hinges on the frame brought him back to lucidity. Seeing it in the hospital was one thing, but watching him hallucinating in my own home, when I was responsible for him, was completely different.

That morning I watched him in his chair, eyes closed, his hands grasping phantom food as he brought them to his open mouth, chewing slowly, clearly savoring his snack. Even with the gravity of the situation, I couldn't help teasing him a little bit.

"Hey Papa . . . what are you eating?" I asked him. His blue eyes slowly opened and focused on me, starting to clear behind his glasses.

"Oh, just this sandwich."

"Sandwich? Where is it?" Confused by my question, he slowly looked down at his empty hands, then checked his chest and lap for any crumbs.

"Oh. I must have finished it," he concluded, with an air of finality.

Later that day, with my father home early from work, I headed upstairs to take a nap. With my dad on caretaker duty downstairs, Papa began dreaming he was on the toilet, when he was still in his living-room. His pants were already around his ankles before my dad shook him awake and averted disaster. Soon thereafter, I woke to the sound of my father's heavy footsteps thudding up the stairs. I was rolling out of bed by the time he reached the door, and seeing the expression on my dad's face as he burst in, I feared the worst.

Papa had fallen in the bathroom. Bursting through the open bathroom door, I was greeted by two slipper-clad feet dangling out of the bathtub, like Dorothy's first view in Oz. Plaid pajama pants were wrapped around his ankles, bunched over the ever-present, knee-high compression socks. An incongruous pink towel was rolled up and wedged behind his head. From his expression he could have been laying back in a comfy recliner instead of an unforgiving ceramic tub. I quickly scanned his body and, aside from a tiny trickle of blood down his leg, could see nothing obviously wrong. This wasn't altogether reassuring, as the possibility of a broken bone, concussion, or split-open sternum was very real. With my dad crowded behind me in the tiny bathroom, I edged closer to Papa, sure I was about to be calling an ambulance. "Hey Papa," I said in the same reassuring voice I would have used with a skittish animal, "how are you feeling?" He seemed completely lucid and slightly bemused by my concern when he answered my questions, saying that he hadn't hit his head and didn't feel pain anywhere else. He had a small puncture wound where his thigh had snagged the protruding edge of the little plastic guide that keeps the shower doors in place, but that seemed to be his only injury.

My dad was unable to extricate Papa from his position wedged crossways in the bathtub. When dealing with an octogenarian whose rib cage was split with a bone saw less than a month ago, caution is merited. He wasn't supposed to raise his arms above his shoulders, and I was relieved my dad hadn't taken his hand and tried to pull him to his feet. Even though he had shrunk with age, Papa was not a little man, and I could see why my father was stumped as to how to disentangle him. Finally, I stood in the tub myself, wrapped my arms under Papa's and hoisted him to his feet, all while attempting not to put any strain on his injured chest or glance down and see the source of one-quarter of my genetic material. I held him there for a long second, letting him find his balance, afraid he would collapse again or discover a new injury, but he seemed uncharacteristically steady.

How he didn't break a hip, slam his head back against the wall, or try to catch himself with an arm and wrench open his injured chest cavity remains a mystery. After we got him safely back to bed, I ran several slow-motion reenactments of what must have happened, without being able to shed any light on how he was unharmed. After seeing Papa helpless in the tub the thought crept in, for the first time, that he might not make it back home.

CHAPTER 8

Starvation Fare

The food ration of prisoners of war shall be equivalent in quantity and quality to that of the depot troops. Prisoners shall also be afforded the means of preparing for themselves such additional articles of food as they may possess. Sufficient drinking water shall be supplied to them. The use of tobacco shall be authorized. Prisoners may be employed in the kitchens.

All collective disciplinary measures affecting food are prohibited.
—ARTICLE 11, GENEVA CONVENTION, 1929

Dec 27: One cup of soup—lousy.
—ROBERT COZEAN, PRISON DIARY, 1944

IN MY GRANDFATHER'S PRISON, HUNGER AND COLD WERE THE true enemies, not the Germans. As their bodies burned precious calories to stay warm, each man would split a small loaf of bitter black bread with five other prisoners. After his one-sixth share of bread, each would receive a cup of watery soup; the menu alternated between pea-, rice-, and potato-flavored liquid. Grass was often used in the soup as well, and most men were sick from it. The one constant was the water content—the prisoners would joke that the cook dropped the pea into the soup on a string so they could pull it up and use it again for the next batch.

The foul black bread that was served was known as *"Kriegs-brot,"* which translates as war-bread. The recipe, as quoted from the records of the German Food Providing Ministry published in Berlin in 1941, was "50% bruised rye grain, 20% sliced sugar beets, 20% 'tree flour' (sawdust), 10% minced leaves and straw."

Prisoners often reported finding sand or glass in the bread, but their hunger was so great they ate it anyway. The men had different philosophies about their daily rations. Some chose to eat their daily allotment all at once. This eliminated the risk of it being lost, dropped, or stolen, but left them with nothing until the next meal. Characteristically, Papa chose to slowly nibble on the bread throughout the day. It gave him something to look forward to, a hope that perhaps the aching of hunger would be quieted a bit during the night—though that hope would go unfulfilled, night after night.

The men drew straws to see who would cut the loaf of bread each day. The man who cut it would get the last slice, after the other five men had chosen, so he had to cut carefully. Sometimes it would take half an hour to slice the bread as evenly as possible. The tiny loaf would be cut in half, then again into thirds. Every crumb was scooped up and consumed.

The Army intelligence report on Stalag IXB reads: "The German rations had a paper value of 1400 calories. Actually, the caloric content was even further lowered by the waste in using products of inferior quality. Since a completely inactive man needs at least 1700 calories to live, it is apparent that PW

[Prisoners of War] were slowly starving to death." The Germans weren't entirely uncivilized with their menu, providing a cauldron of tea as well. Unfortunately, they used unclean water for the tea that was, according to my grandfather, guaranteed to have you camped on the latrine for several days. The men did appreciate the tea—they used it for hot water to wash their faces and shave.

Bowls and utensils weren't provided to the POWs, so the men ate out of what they could find. Many used their helmets as bowls for the soup. Papa had scrounged a metal tin he used throughout his captivity.

When the Americans first arrived at Stalag IXB, the Russian prisoners of war were in charge of the kitchen detail, given only rotted vegetables to use in the soup. The resulting rations were inedible. A German officer, Hauptmann Kuhle, allowed the Americans to replace the Russians in the kitchen, an act of kindness that saved hundreds of lives. Oatmeal was substituted for the putrid vegetables, and under American supervision, the food improved. In another act of kindness, a German guard, Pvt. Dathe, allowed the kitchen detail to steal eight bushels of potatoes to distribute to the men, preventing outright starvation.

Food was also used to keep the prisoners in line—a direct violation of the Geneva Convention's directive, "All collective disciplinary measures involving food are prohibited." Papa told me about one POW who, unable to take the hunger gnawing at his stomach any longer, snuck into the kitchen in hopes of stealing some bread or perhaps a potato, and was caught by a guard. The prisoner knocked the guard down and sprinted out into the night. The camp authorities told the men they wouldn't receive any food until the man gave himself up, or was identified and turned in by the other prisoners. When the men refused to betray their comrade, the entire camp, already half-starved, went without food for more than twenty-four hours. Finally the chaplain went to the man and begged him to confess, for the sake of the rest of the POWs. When he did, the guards took him out into the woods, intending to shoot him. There was a rumor that he had run from the firing squad and escaped—all the prisoners knew was that he never returned.

With their empty stomachs aching, food dominated conversation. What's the first thing you're going to eat when we get out of here? To drink? What about for breakfast? Steak and potatoes or salmon and rice? These mythological menus gained complexity with each day spent in captivity. My grandfather wrote—on precious, pilfered paper—two things while he was imprisoned. The first was a brief diary, scrawled onto a single page, missing many days and consisting of only two- or three-word entries. The second was a full, four-page folding menu, every inch on the front and back inscribed with the food he was going to indulge in after his rescue. When he unfolded it for me, he laughed, "I was going to eat five meals a day, for the next six months."

Under the section "Three Main Meals" Papa had recorded his choices for his first, second, and third meals after he was liberated, for breakfast, lunch, and dinner. He even planned out what he would take on the train home, and it would have been more than he ate during his entire stay in Stalag IXB: one dozen donuts, six éclairs, six cream puffs, one cake, one pie, and six hamburgers.

His friend Charles wrote about his ideal menu, "For breakfast I pined for pineapple juice, Wheaties with bananas or strawberries, bacon and three eggs, six slices of toast with strawberry jam, a short order of waffles with sorghum and sausage, topped off by several cups of coffee," and for lunch he was looking forward to french fries and fried chicken.

Even the tiny diary that my grandfather kept was mostly concerned with food. Some of his entries:

Jan. 10	*Soup like water*
Jan. 18	*Traded for a couple potatoes*
Jan. 23	*Got a carrot and potato*
Jan. 28	*Guard was hit in kitchen. No church, no food till the one gives up*
Feb. 8	*Bread soup, no good*
Feb. 10	*Potato soup—got a haircut*
Feb. 11	*Bread soup—got a piece of meat (trade) for it.*
Feb. 21	*Potato soup, thick*
Mar. 14	*Grit soup, got part of Red Cross box*

Doctors at prisoner of war conventions have told the POWs that their culinary fantasies kept their gastric juices flowing and prevented them from developing long-term stomach problems. But I think these discussions were even more important for the hope of rescue they implied. Each conversation about a future delicacy back home assumed survival, a prospect that must have seemed bleak as the snows piled up and they watched their ribs grow more prominent.

A few weeks into his imprisonment, the guards allowed my grandfather to fill out a Red Cross POW postcard that they would send home. It combined sentimentality with the need to survive, as he maintained hope that a package of food would arrive. The postcard also showed that his dream of building a house upon his return was alive and well.

T-House
No of VINE / 3 MAIN MEALS

BREAKFAST | LUNCH | DINNERS ON BACK
① POST TOASTIES | ① CREAM Tomato soup |
with BANANAS | LETTUCE Tomato EGG |
EGGS AND BACON | PORK CHOPS | TAKE ON TRAM
Toast BUTTER JELLY | MASHED POTATOES | 1 DOZ DONUTS
PAN CAKES or WAFFLE | BUTTERED CORN | 6 ECLAIRS
COFFEE and COFFEE CAKE | CLOVER ROLLS | 6 CREAM PUFFS
 | BUTTER | 1 CAKE
② | MILK | 1 PIE
PINEAPPLE JUICE | ChocLATE Pudding | 6 HAMBURGERS
OATS | ANGEL Food CAKE | 3 CHEESE
FRENCH TOAST | | 3 HAM
PORK SAUSAGE | ② POTATO SOUP | COLD LUNCH
PRUNES | PINEAPPLE CHEESE | COLD MEATS
COFFEE DONUTS | VEAL CUTLETS | SPAM, ham
 | BAKED POTATOES | LIVERWURST
③ GRAPEFRUIT | STRING BEANS | CHEESE BOLOGNA
HAM AND EGGS | BUTTERED CARROTS | POTATO SALAD
Hot BISCUITS | PARKER House ROLLS | DEVILED EGGS
BUTTER JELLY | BUTTER | PhILED FISH,
COFFEE | MILK | CHEESE
CIMMON ROLLS | Hot MINCE PIE | OLIVES, PICKL,
 | | ONIONS Rad ish
✓ SNACKS | | CELERY
 | | POTATO CHIPS
TUNA ON TOAST | ③ CLAM Chowder Soup | FRUIT JELLO
CHEESE ON RYE | LETTUCE SALAD | WHIP CREAM ICE CREAM
RITZ CRACKERS | FRENCH DRESSING |
PEANUT BUTTER | RAINBOW TROUT |
STRAWBERRY SHORT CAKE | MACARONI |
FROSTED MALKS | CORN MUFFINS |
CREAM PUFFS | MILK, Butter Sex Puste |

The top three choices for breakfast, lunch, and dinner were all listed on the front pages, while the back pages were devoted to a shopping list to be filled upon his return.

DINNER

① SHRIMP COCKTAIL
CHICKEN NOODLE SOUP
LETTUCE AVACADO SALAD
BOWL CELERY OLIVES
ONIONS RADISHES PICKLES
SPAGHETTI AND CHEESE
    CHOICE   SWISS
    OF   SIRLOIN
    STEAKS   T-BONE
             ROUND
             HAMBURGER
    FRENCH FRYS
    LIMA BEANS
    CREAM PEAS
    BUTTER BEETS
    FRENCH ROLLS
    BUTTER
    COFFEE
    APPLE PIE
    ALAMODE
    CANDIES

② HERRING COCKTAIL
VEGETABLE SOUP
MIXED SALAD
BAKED VA. HAM
CANDIED YAMS
BLACK EYES PEAS
CORN ON THE COB
WHOLE WHEAT
BREAD BUTTER
COFFEE
HOT FUDGE SUNDEA
CHOCLATE CAKE

③ FRUIT COCKTAIL
CHICKEN SOUP
PEAR CHEESE SALAD
BOWL CELERY OLIVES
ONIONS RADISHES PICKLE
CHOICE CHICKEN
OF   TURKEY
        RABBITT
DUMPLINGS
MASHED POTATOES
SWEET POTATOES
BUTTER PEAS
CRANBERRY SAUCE
HOT BISCUITS
MILK GRAVEY
PUMPKIN PIE
WHIPPED CREAM
ODD AND ENDS
MEAT LOAF
WIENERS
SALMON STEAKS
SPARE RIBS
LAMB CHOPS
ROAST BEEF
ROAST PORK
BELL PEPPER
MEAT BALL
SPAGETTI

January 9, 1945
Dearest Kitty:
Well sweets I can write a few more lines. Send me a package,
the same stuff as before. I am all right. Send lots of sugar. I
have been thinking about building our home. I have built it
over and over again. *Tell your folks hello and I'm thinking
of you more each day and a million kisses to you and lots of
Love—Bob*

When the calendar turned to February, the guards again
allowed the prisoners to write home on POW postcards. It would
be the last letter he wrote during his stay as a guest of the German Army, and his thoughts again turned to the hope of surviving the camp and returning to his wife.

February 1, 1945
Dearest Kitty:
*Well sweets I can write again the old month has passed by.
I only hope they keep on going like that as sweets I miss you
more and more and every day that passes means I am one day
closer to you. Honey I always think of you and a million kisses
and lots of Love—Bob*

During the 103 days of captivity, Papa didn't receive a single
letter or package from home. He did split part of a Red Cross box
with men in his barracks on March 14th, two and a half months
after entering Stalag IXB. That would be his sole respite from a
soup and black bread diet during his time as a POW.

My grandfather lost sixty pounds, emerging a gaunt, skeletal
parody of the vibrant young man who had gone to war. Papa had

one advantage in the prison camp—he didn't smoke. In the camps, cigarettes were the only currency, and more valuable than gold. Every week a group of men were detailed as a work crew to unload the potato wagon bringing supplies for the guards, and maybe one lonely potato to dip up and down into the prisoners' soup. These lucky few would wear overalls and fill their pockets with ten or twelve potatoes, which they would trade. My grandfather had two packs, distributed to his company before he left for the front lines and hidden from the guards. He used them sparingly throughout his imprisonment, occasionally purchasing a potato from a nicotine-addicted member of the potato wagon detail.

Papa spoke of putting the potato on the hot metal of the stove, watching it with the intensity reserved for a starving man surrounded by other starving men. He waited only until it was half cooked before gingerly plucking it from the impromptu grill and eating it. Throughout his life he enjoyed eating baked potatoes. I'm sure his experiences during the war gave him a greater appreciation of cooking his lunch in the microwave and being able to add butter and sour cream.

I would have assumed, with its scarcity and importance, that food would be hoarded by the prisoners, and fights would break out over scraps of bread or a rare potato. But the stories my grandfather related disabused me of those notions. When Charles was sick and couldn't hold down any food, he gave my grandfather half of his meager allotment of soup. After his friend recovered, my grandfather repaid his debt, giving up half his rations to allow Charles to regain his strength. The two of them worked together, never wavering in their determination to survive, even as the German guards enjoyed the Red Cross rations sent for them, citing "transportation breakdowns."

Chapter 9

In Need of a Tune-Up

"I don't know if I should tell him this," Papa said from the passenger seat as we pulled up to the curb at the USC University Hospital for the appointment with his heart surgeon.

"What's that?"

"That I came in here a man, and left a cripple." The tone was dispassionate, but I was shocked by the bitterness and anger that boiled in his words.

"Papa, if you hadn't had the surgery, you would probably already be on the wrong side of the lawn!" I protested. He just harrumphed and looked away as I got the walker from the trunk, clearly not wanting to continue the conversation or hear my defense of the surgeon he was blaming for his present condition.

I was even more stunned because getting him to his appointment had been the goal in front of me, ever since he began to regress. I had thought of us as a team, working together to get him better. But where I had seen this day as a finish line, for him it was just another doctor's appointment—a reminder that he was further from his goal than he had been before the surgeon cut into him. It was the first time I had heard anything like despair from my grandfather.

Because the appointment was at 9:30 in the morning, during the heart of rush hour traffic, it gave Papa and my dad the challenge of figuring out the quickest route to the hospital. After they had mapped out a route with about six freeway changes, I suggested that Papa and I drive up the afternoon before and spend the night at his house. Papa eagerly supported the idea, anxious to be back in his own bed. I was hoping to break the monotony of his recovery, but was concerned both by the logistical difficulties of getting him up the stairs and by assuming total responsibility for him for more than twenty-four hours. Then I realized it didn't matter whether we were at my house, his house, or in the car—Papa was dependent on me. His excitement convinced me it was worth the risk. The first challenge was apparent as soon as we arrived: getting him up his steep driveway. I didn't want to simply pull up as far as I could, because then Papa would be exiting the car on uneven, sloping ground. On the other hand, if I parked on the street he couldn't possible summit his driveway under his own power, even with my supporting hand on his back providing a boost. I wasn't sure his pride or his rib cage would survive being hoisted over my shoulder and carried inside, so my typical engineering problem-solving mantra—brute force and ignorance—was useless too.

With an apologetic pat on the dashboard of my trusty 1997 Subaru station wagon, I shifted into first and revved the engine. My feet dancing on the accelerator and clutch, we managed the thin line between crashing through the garage door and sliding back down the steep grade. For the first time in my life I wished I drove an automatic, but eventually the space between my front bumper and the garage door disappeared.

Now for the tricky part—I had decided the easiest thing to do would be to turn the car sideways in the driveway, letting Papa lean back against the car as he got out and making his walk inside as short as possible. A couple of neighbors halted their walks to watch the show as I began turning the wheel, basically trying to parallel park up against his house. To his credit, Papa remained silent throughout the procedure, though he did occasionally chuckle at some of the choice comments I muttered under my breath. When I finally yanked the emergency brake, the car was almost perpendicular to the driveway, just far enough away from the garage for Papa to open his door.

I came around to help Papa out of the car, and he leaned back against it before heading for the railings on the side entrance and climbing up the four steps. He was left gasping for air after the exertion and leaned back against the railing, trying to catch his breath, as I retrieved his walker.

As Papa rested, his longtime neighbor Ray came out to check on us. Ray was a retired firefighter, short and stocky with a thatch of white hair. He and Papa had lived next to each other for at least forty years, and had grown very close after my grandmother passed away. In a cost-cutting scheme worthy of their generation, they would even share a copy of the morning paper. It was always comforting to my parents, with Papa living alone, that Ray was next door.

The three of us talked for a few minutes, filling Ray in on the medical developments of the last few weeks. Papa confidently announced that he would be back in the house for good in a week or so—a goal I thought was clearly unrealistic, but without that hope, what did he have left? His confidence in surviving never seemed to waiver, even as the obstacles mounted. Perhaps that was a legacy of his time in the POW camp—the feeling that after he had survived World War II and Stalag IXB, everything else was child's play. It didn't seem like false confidence either; he had an appointment with his eye doctor to remove a cataract scheduled for the next week and steadily resisted any suggestion that he might want to call and postpone. He had also booked a vacation out to Palm Springs with the Girls in February, which he mentioned often. As our conversation wound down and Ray headed home, Papa turned and squared his shoulders, preparing for the next challenge, twenty feet of uphill walking to reach four more steps and finally his back door.

We started up the narrow cement walkway, my hand still resting on his lower back. About halfway up his walker slipped off the path into the dirt and Papa suddenly toppled over. Fortunately he fell in my direction and, instead of tumbling into the dirt on the other side, he leaned into me. Instinctively my hand slid around his back and I braced, catching his weight with my shoulder. We stood there for a second, and I could feel his chest heaving. Gently I stood him back up and replaced his walker onto the cement and we continued, without a word being exchanged.

Once we made it into the house everything was as he had left it, but nothing was the same. All I could see was how treacherous his familiar confines could be. He couldn't sit in his favorite broken-in recliner because it would have been impossible for him to get out. The stairs leading down to the basement, pool table, and garage were absolutely out of the question. Papa had confessed, after finally putting a railing by those steep stairs, that he often had to crawl up the last few steps to open the door, even before his heart problems. The hallway, which had always been far too tight and narrow for two people to pass each other in, was barely wide enough to accommodate his walker, and I worried about him slamming his fingers against the walls on either side. Even the tiny lip between the carpet of his dining room and the linoleum of the kitchen loomed as a tripping hazard. As excited as Papa was to be able to sleep in his own bed, it could hardly have been the homecoming he was anticipating.

When I learned we would be at his house that night, I gave the Girls, Pat and Mary, a call, asking them to come over for dinner. I didn't want to leave Papa alone at the house to go to the store, so I asked them to pick something up for us on the way over. That was a mistake. They eventually arrived—after an interminable debate on the phone over which restaurant to go to—and brought in food in plastic boxes. Given the choice, I think the boxes might have tasted better than their contents. My meal was allegedly fish and chips, although it was hard to tell which was which. Papa, evidently conditioned by prison camp food and my cooking, scarfed down whatever was masquerading as steak with a smile on his face.

As bad as the meal was, I was happy that Papa could have a normal night back home. A bit of the old sparkle returned to his eyes as he got to flirt with his lady friends, accepting their kisses on his cheek and good-natured complaints about the scratchiness of his mustache, which he had been letting grow. It reminded me of an old photo he had saved, taken in Paris, of him after his liberation. His face had aged and wrinkled, but his eyes and the mustache looked exactly the same.

After dinner I hooked him up to his mobile oxygen tank and cleared the trash, trying to avoid as much of their conversation as I could. As far as I could tell, it consisted of long, drawn-out accounts of the doings of the church Bible study and updates about who was newly in or out of the hospital. They weren't sure what had happened to one of Papa's friends, who had suffered a severe stroke. Probably in a nursing home somewhere, they agreed, and Papa just nodded, as if that was an acceptable answer. After that, Mary segued into discussing retirement home options for Papa—which is when I promptly ushered them both out. "Early appointment tomorrow . . . need some sleep . . . thanks for the stuff, er, food . . . great to see you . . . watch your step on the stairs . . . goodnight."

We sat at the kitchen table in a heavy silence for a few more minutes after they left, the same table where I had first interviewed him months before. I was furious; I had invited the Girls over to give him one nice, normal evening in the midst of his long recovery, thinking that getting back to a routine dinner with them would give Papa hope and confidence that he could regain the life he had before surgery. Instead, Mary thought it was the proper time to babble on about Invalid Gardens and Old-Folks Estates. Everyone in the family knew that was a possibility, but by unspoken agreement we had never mentioned it. Having to sell the house would be devastating to Papa, both the loss of the property he had designed, built, and raised a family in, but more importantly as an admission that he was no longer capable of living an independent life.

He sighed heavily, and looked more tired in that moment than I had ever seen him. "What do you think?" he asked.

I deliberately let some of the anger into my voice, "Papa, I think it's incredibly stupid to talk about any of this before you see the doctor tomorrow. If he's still hopeful about your recovery, there's no reason we can't get you back here." I stood, patting him on the back as I cleaned the last of the dishes from the table. "Let's get you to bed. Big day tomorrow."

I walked him down the narrow hallway to his room and got him settled in bed, with the pee bottle in easy reach on the nightstand, and leaving his door open when I headed to my room.

The next morning I woke to the sound of a walker skidding down the hallway outside my room. I had brought up a half-gallon of milk and some cereal, and I prepared two bowls for us, topping them with sugar. As we ate, I noticed Papa seemed much older than he had the night before. The activity of the previous day had clearly drained his strength and, while he was happy to have woken up in his own bed, I could tell he was already dreading the walk down to the car. Or perhaps he was fearful of the news he would get from the doctor. I was approaching his appointment as the completion of a mission, but for him the jury was about to return a verdict.

Going downhill and downstairs proved to be much easier than the climb up. After I extricated us from his driveway, Papa was in his element, giving both directions and a history lesson as we took surface streets through Pasadena and downtown L.A. It seemed like every street we crossed had a story. Down one street was his mother's old house. He told me how she got so crazy at the end of her life she kept the blinds drawn and the house so dark that she had no idea what time it was, calling her family members at three in the morning. She would also occasionally brandish a shotgun at family, neighbors, or costumed kids on Halloween. No one seemed that concerned, until she passed away and they discovered it had been loaded the whole time. On other streets he remembered old stores or offices, long since out of business, that had ordered carpentry work from his shop. Another road led to the baseball diamond where he had played second base on the church softball team. After about thirty minutes—the most normal half hour we had spent together since his surgery—we arrived at the hospital.

I helped him to the bench in front of the doctor's office, parked the car, and returned to help him into the elevator. He was so unsteady I began leaving my hand on his back continuously, giving him support and a little extra stability. I noticed that I got more looks from attractive young nurses than usual when I was with my grandfather, usually accompanied by an approving smile. I was finally getting payback for those tennis matches he had taken me to as a kid.

After heading all the way up to the fifth floor, we found the office of his surgeon. Papa slumped down, exhausted, as I talked to the receptionist from behind the high walls that barricaded her off from the waiting room. I thought her voice sounded familiar, but I wasn't sure she was the one who had brushed me off on the phone. She demanded to know if we had gotten his chest X-ray done and seemed personally affronted when I told her we hadn't, because no one in her office had bothered mentioning it. I refused to leave her desk, much less go all the way back down to the ground floor for an X-ray, until she got us a wheelchair. Looking over my shoulder at Papa, hunched over and struggling to breathe, she reluctantly assented.

I was feeling pretty good about my victory, but she got the last laugh. The wheelchair they scrounged up was either designed for a sumo wrestler or a family of four. I've got a pretty good wingspan, but I struggled to reach the wide-set handles. The wheelchair was about four inches thinner than the hallways we were traversing, so anyone trying to head the other direction was straight out of luck. We had the iron foot pedals out and were moving at ramming speed, sending doctors, nurses, and interns scurrying the other way or into doorways, fleeing for their shins. The wheelchair was so wide that I entertained the notion of sitting down next to Papa, each of us pushing one wheel for locomotion, though in his weakened state we would just end up going in circles.

After his chest X-ray we headed back up to the fifth floor and, after the customary wait, we were shown into the exam room. Papa was first examined by a nurse with a stethoscope, and then by his surgeon, accompanied by a small, mousy medical student who clung to the background and seemed out of place next to the hard-charging doctor. Papa was still breathing heavily, with a slight wheeze, and was not entirely lucid, so I had to answer most of their questions. After peering at the X-ray with the appearance of spontaneity, pretending he hadn't just been reviewing it in his office, the surgeon announced that the combination of fluid build-up in the lungs and his bulging feet indicated a fluid imbalance that he thought best corrected by a "tune-up" back in the hospital.

A wave of relief washed over me, as someone in the medical community finally acknowledged the problem. He had been seen daily by nurses, who talked about more food and rest, when he really needed a hospital bed. The doctor's assessment was a confirmation that my concerns were valid, and I was finally able to get him into the hands of someone who could help. Speaking to the nurse later, she told me Papa had looked so sick that she started the paperwork to get him a hospital bed even before the surgeon had seen him.

I was relieved; Papa was devastated. His eyes assumed the frightened, frenetic movements of a prisoner looking for an exit. The examining room was packed tightly with the doctor, nurse, and medical student, prison guards armed with well-practiced looks of sincerity and compassion. Seeing his panicked look, I asked if we could have a minute, and we discussed his options. Trying to improve his outlook, I asked a question that I would repeat, in various forms, until we got him checked into the hospital several hours later: "Isn't this the best news we could have gotten? Yeah, it's too bad that you have to be back in the hospital, but it's just for a few days. At least what is wrong is fixable!"

This seemed to revive him, the idea of a finite period of imprisonment and a hope for real recovery, and I helped him start making plans for after his release, trying to get his mind off his impending stay in the hospital. We sat together in the waiting room for several hours, until they found an empty room and moved him in. As I was leaving for the night, a pretty Filipina nurse entered his room and the last thing I heard as I walked out the door was, "You know, I served in World War II...."

CHAPTER 10

Lucky . . . for a POW

Prisoners of war shall be lodged in buildings or huts which afford all possible safeguards as regards hygiene and salubrity. The premises must be entirely free from damp, and adequately heated and lighted. All precautions shall be taken against the danger of fire. As regards dormitories, their total area, minimum cubic air space, fittings and bedding material, the conditions shall be the same as for the depot troops of the detaining Power.
—ARTICLE 10, GENEVA CONVENTION, 1929

"Dec 30: Got cold—slept back to back."
—ROBERT COZEAN, PRISON DIARY, 1944

THE MOST FRIGHTENING MOMENT FOR PAPA IN THE CAMP wasn't a result of starvation, and it wasn't the moment his barracks were strafed. My grandfather could feel his body wasting away, but he still had the day's rations and the chance of getting a potato or piece of cheese to sustain hope. And the strafing happened too quickly to be frightening—it was over in a heartbeat, and you were left either dead or alive. The most terrifying incident in Stalag IXB had to do with the cold.

131

More than halfway through their captivity, desperate prisoners attempted another raid on the kitchen. They were surprised by two German guards and attacked them, somehow killing both. All the men in the camp were pulled from their barracks and forced to stand on the parade ground until the guilty prisoners confessed or were identified. A POW noted the temperature in his diary: 1.5 degrees below freezing. The men, most without coats, stood before the machine guns on a hill as the wind whipped through them.

They were held there for six hours in the sub-freezing temperatures. Men began falling to the ground, dragged back to their feet by their friends. Finally the guards discovered bloody clothes in a barracks, and two prisoners were hauled away. The remaining men leaned on each other for strength and warmth, staggering back to the scant shelter of the barracks, so thankful to still be alive they didn't even mind missing their day's meager rations. The perpetrators weren't seen again.

During that ordeal, or perhaps simply from prolonged exposure to the cold, Papa's legs became frostbitten. Ever since his time in the prison camp, no hair has grown on his legs. I discovered this after his surgery, when I was putting on his compression socks. When I asked him about it, he told me the reason, adding "If I could figure out how to do that again, I could make a million dollars on them women."

The average high in January at the site of Stalag IXB is 37°F, and the low is well below freezing. That winter was one of the harshest that any of the locals could remember. The record low for the region is six degrees below zero. During the heart of winter it typically snows, sleets, or rains every other day in Bad Orb.

At night, when the temperature plunged even further, the wood in the stove was the only protection from the cold. The men had barely enough to burn for one hour during the coldest part of the night. The only exception was when the Red Cross representative visited the camp to report on conditions for the men. Then German guards stacked full buckets of coal by the stoves. The POWs were threatened with death if they touched the coal, which gave the illusion that the barracks were heated. The guards would also put temporary patches over the worst of the holes in the walls and windows. Like the coal, these disappeared as soon as the Red Cross representative was out of sight. Papa and Charles survived the nights by huddling back to back and covering themselves with both blankets.

On the same day my grandfather entered the gates of Stalag IXB, his father, not knowing of Papa's capture, wrote him a letter that would be returned to sender. It's probably for the best, as I'm not sure my grandfather would have been very sympathetic about his father having to go without breakfast, considering on the day the letter was written Papa had eaten one meal in the prior eight days and survived by scooping up dirty snow from the side of the road.

December 26, 1944
Dear Robert:
This year will soon be gone, just the balance of this week, and then 1945 will appear on the letters, etc. It has been a year that will long be remembered by many, and one that we will all want to forget. I am taking your advice and have decided to go and get fixed up physically. Last week I decided that I had carried this sore side of mine long enough and went to the doctor. Of course he wanted an Xray of everything I had from the top

of my head to my big toe. I went out Wednesday for this perfor-
mance and his first order was to appear at the Xray room with-
out any breakfast or even a drink of water at 9 a.m. For my
breakfast they gave me a glass of "barium" which they watched
go down with the fluoroscope. On an empty stomach I went
down too. I passed out with a sick stomach. They laid me down
and continued to look. They took 8 or ten pictures and ordered
me to return at 3 p.m. with still nothing to eat or nothing to
drink. Believe me that last two hours were torture . . . We sure
do appreciate getting the picture. I cannot say that I like it. Of
course we wanted it, but I like you better without the uniform.
With Love,
Dad and Mom

As Papa was trying to adjust to life in the prison camp, his family, back in sunny Southern California, was still writing letters, unaware he was in German hands. The letters, returned by the Army, were saved, and show the disconnect between Papa and his wife—a disconnect that would continue even after he returned from the war, when she was still unable to understand what he had been through.

December 27, 1944
Darling Bob,
Good morning and how are you this nice cold morning? Fine,
I hope. It is really cold here this morning and I'm not just
a kidding. It is sure cold in the engineering department too.
Don't know where this heat is but it sure isn't here!! Lots of
Love,
Kitty

January 4, 1945
Darling Bob,
When I started this letter, I didn't have any news but I just had the urge to talk to you. Boy this is a heck of a life we are leading, darling. But anyway we have each other and that is what counts, isn't it?

The weather has certainly been beautiful since the New Year, just like spring, so nice and sunny and warm.
Kitty

Even after learning of Papa's capture, Kitty and his parents continued to send letters, hoping the Red Cross would be able to deliver them, and focusing on hope for the future.

March 14, 1945
Dear Robert:
We came home, and then had a bite of supper, and then I took Kitty home. We sat in the car and talked about an hour before she went in. Talking about . . . Well, you should know. Your plans for the future. The house etc. You have a great little wife waiting for you. Sure was a relief to see your handwriting again. Up to date she has received two cards, and one letter, dated Jan. 5, 6, and 9th. They come thru pretty good, considering the distance, and the way they have to travel to get back here . . .

Just as soon as Kitty gets the permit for mailing the package to you, she will send you the extra package. We told her that we would like to share in sending the package, as she is the only one that can send one, and she is limited to one 11 pound package every sixty days, which will come thru the

Red Cross. Believe me all is being done, as fast as it can be done to get one on the road to you . . .

We are all anxiously waiting the day of your return, and are praying for you constantly. Until that day remember you have a little wife working and waiting, as a good soldier's wife should be, and then you can pick up where you and her left off with your plans for the future.
With Love,
Dad and Mom

———

It seems obscene to call someone lucky who was force-marched across Belgium, herded onto a boxcar for five days, starved into losing sixty pounds, held at attention in subfreezing temperatures for six hours, and suffered through a brutal German winter with just a threadbare, lice-infested Army uniform. But my grandfather was fortunate—at least by the standards of POWs. America's wars, in general, have not been kind to those taken captive.

The history of American POWs is longer than the history of America itself; the first prisoners that can be considered American, instead of colonial Englishmen, were captured nearly a year before the Declaration of Independence was signed. During the course of the Revolutionary War thirty-two thousand Americans were taken prisoner, more than four times the number killed in battle. Many of these captives were held in New York, which remained under British control for most of the war. Without space to house them in the city, POWs were loaded onto ships anchored in the bay. Stories from these floating prisons rival the most horrible atrocities of World War II. The most infamous, the HMS *Jersey*, held eleven hundred prisoners, three times the number of sailors it was designed to support. Jammed into the holds, the men were slowly starved to death, receiving only eight ounces of "condemned" bread and a pint of water daily—basically equivalent to the rations Papa received in Stalag IXB.

Although estimates vary, historians believe as many as eighteen thousand patriots died in captivity during the Revolutionary War, far more than those who died on the battlefield. More than half of those that surrendered didn't survive. Papa was captured almost two hundred years after those men, but faced the same trials—starvation, disease, filth, and unbearable weather.

In general, conditions were far better for prisoners during the Civil War, at least for the first few years of conflict. Both the Confederate and Union governments formed an agreement to trade prisoners, saving them the difficulties of having to house captured soldiers. Even if the other side didn't have prisoners to trade, a prisoner was paroled within ten days. He would sign a pledge not to fight until his own army paroled one of their prisoners in exchange. Being paroled was often the best thing that could happen to a soldier—he had loyally served his country, but was honor-bound not to take up arms again and get shot at again he was formally exchanged. There are even reports of soldiers deliberately allowing themselves to be captured, knowing they would be paroled and not required to fight anymore.

Everything changed in 1863, when the parole system broke down. Initially the failure, like the war itself, was over slavery. Confederate leaders stated that black Union soldiers who were captured would be treated as escaped slaves. This was unacceptable to the Union, and in response prisoner exchanges ceased. Later in the war, General Ulysses S. Grant refused to offer prisoner exchanges because the North had mobilized much greater manpower than the South. With his overwhelming numerical superiority, Grant knew his armies could withstand the loss of their prisoners, while depriving the Confederate Army of their captured soldiers would have a much greater effect. With the Union armies destroying farms and cities throughout the South, any paroled Confederate would immediately take up arms to protect his home, regardless of any oath that had been sworn. By refusing parole for captured soldiers, Grant believed that the war could be shortened.

When the prisoner exchanges ceased, both the North and South were unprepared to provide food or shelter for the massive number of captured soldiers, resulting in starvation and rampant disease in hastily formed prison camps. Perhaps the worst of these was located in Andersonville, Georgia.

The camp, designed to hold ten thousand men, was overflowing with thirty-two thousand captured Union troops. Diseases swept through the crowded and malnourished men, and nearly one-third died. Yet unlike conditions during the Revolutionary War or for Papa and his fellow POWs in World War II, the poor conditions were not deliberate—the South didn't have the resources to feed their own troops either. The guards and POWs were given the same fare. The Confederate government even reported the terrible conditions to General Grant, informing him they were unable to feed and house the prisoners and asking him to exchange prisoners for them. Grant refused, unwilling to risk allowing any captured Confederate soldier to rejoin the fighting, and the Union troops held in Andersonville suffered for his decision.

America's next major war was the first without a large number of captured soldiers. Of the five million troops who went to

Europe to fight in World War I, only 4,120 ended up in enemy hands and 147 died in captivity. For the most part these prisoners received much better treatment than they would in the next war. This was the first conflict when a standard was given for treatment of prisoners and neutral countries and the Red Cross monitored treatment of the POWs.

During World War II, if you had to be captured, it was much better to surrender in Europe than in the Pacific. Of the 140,000 Allied forces taken prisoner by the Japanese, 25 percent died in captivity. The most enduring example of the treatment that POWs received from the Japanese is the Bataan Death March.

Hours after the attack on Pearl Harbor, the Japanese Imperial Army launched an all-out invasion of the Philippines. A three-month battle ensued, with the American and Filipino forces cut off from supplies and slowly starving. Approximately seventy-five thousand emaciated U.S. troops finally surrendered to the Japanese. Knowing his men were sick and weak, the commanding American officer offered to use army trucks and vehicles to transport his men directly to the prison camp. The Japanese instead chose to march the battle-weary men, already half-starved and suffering from malaria and dysentery, on foot between sixty and one hundred miles to a prison camp.

The brutality began immediately. Captives were herded onto the main road, where they were force-marched in the sweltering tropical heat and searched for money and valuables. Japanese troops cut off the fingers of American officers to steal their West Point rings. The killings began soon after, too many to count—a captain decapitated with a sword for possessing Japanese money, a lieutenant stabbed with a bayonet for trying to help another man from the ground, shot where he lay—bodies were everywhere along the road. One man tried counting headless U.S. prisoners on the side of the road, hacked and decapitated by Japanese officers. He got to twenty-seven in just a few miles before he couldn't look anymore.

Between three and four hundred Filipino soldiers had their hands tied with telephone wire and were forced to march into a ravine. The officers started on one end of the line with their swords, the enlisted men on the other with their bayonets, as they systematically murdered the bound prisoners. The killing took until nightfall. Two compassionate locals tried to help the prisoners by presenting them with food. They were caught, tied to a stake, and burned to death.

Prisoners who fell were killed. Prisoners who stopped for water were killed. Japanese troops driving the other way on the road threw rocks or swung at the prisoners with bamboo sticks or golf clubs. When they reached the gates of the prison camp, the POWs were again frisked, this time more thoroughly. Possession of anything Japanese—money, souvenirs, weapons—was a death sentence. The Japanese even performed grisly medical experiments on their captives.

The march lasted anywhere from two days to three weeks for the captured men. Of the nearly seventy-five thousand men who surrendered, it is estimated that only fifty-four thousand reached the prison camp. A few escaped, and the rest were killed and left to rot alongside the road.

When the war began to turn against the Japanese, orders came down to prevent any captured soldiers from being liberated. In the Philippines 150 POWs were shoved into air raid shelters which were doused in gas and lit on fire. When a few broke down the door to escape the flames, they were gunned down. The threat to the POWs was a major argument for taking drastic action to bring the war in the Pacific to a quick conclusion.

On August 6, 1945, the first atomic bomb was dropped on Hiroshima, a site chosen in part because it was believed no POWs were housed there. Those killed instantaneously were the lucky ones. Thousands of others spent days in agony dying of radiation poisoning. Three days later, with Japanese leaders still defiant, a second bomb was dropped on Nagasaki, despite the presence of American POWs held in the blast radius. The destruction of the city and its inhabitants finally ended the war and forced the release of the POWs.

Amazingly enough, despite the wretched conditions for Papa at Stalag IXB—the starvation, the sickness, the cold, the lice, the overcrowded barracks, the forced marches and the boxcar rides—the men imprisoned there could still consider themselves fortunate.

The treatment that captured German soldiers received was in stark contrast to the conditions for Papa in Stalag IXB. A total of 655 camps were needed to house the Axis POWs in America, spread out across forty-seven different states. The German POWs were treated in accordance with the articles of the Geneva Convention—warm beds, access to medical care, food equivalent to what our own troops were served. Even the strictures about personal space were followed, with each prisoner given the same amount of room as a member of the U.S. Army received, about forty square feet. At camps in America, the Germans had access to libraries and musical instruments, organized sporting events, and could even take classes for college credit. About one hundred thousand prisoners were even paid to work in private industries, helping to absorb the manpower shortage caused by the war.

Papa and the men trapped in Germany would have killed for a library—the pages could be ripped out and used as toilet paper.

Surprisingly, the greatest danger to the German prisoners was from other captured soldiers. Many of the POW camps were policed by Nazi hard-liners, who would severely punish anything they saw as collusion with the American authorities. Cases of brutality toward fellow prisoners were extremely common—beatings, intimidation, even murder.

Members of the SS and Gestapo, wanted for war crimes, disguised themselves as regular army soldiers in order to escape detection. When it was discovered that many elite members of the SS had a membership tattoo drawn under their left armpits, all prisoners had to raise their arms and be examined. Fourteen members of the SS who murdered American prisoners at Malmedy during the Battle of the Bulge—on the same day and in the same region as the capture of my grandfather—were identified and removed from the camps to stand trial for war crimes.

Many of the German prisoners were shocked when they reached the shores of the United States that much of the "news" they had heard in Germany was false. Nazi propaganda reported that the United States had been heavily bombed by the Luftwaffe. Some even believed the stories that New York had been all but destroyed by heavy bombing raids, and were surprised by the conspicuous lack of craters and ruins.

In an attempt to reduce the hold of Nazism on the prison camps and to dispel as much of the Third Reich propaganda as possible, the American government began a top-secret effort to "reeducate" the German POWs. The hope was to reduce the violence in the camps and create a group of pro-democracy soldiers who could play an important role in the political transition of postwar Germany. The program was kept completely secret until after the surrender of Germany and Allied victory in Europe.

The first phase of the program was exchanging any pro-Nazi literature at the prison libraries for more acceptable books. Fortunately, such a list of books already existed—the ones that had been burned and banned by the Third Reich. The libraries were slowly altered, in what seemed to the prisoners like a normal book rotation, until the material in the libraries was completely changed out. Pamphlets were distributed that gave short summaries of American history and other popular subjects. Local colleges and universities were encouraged to reach out to the camps and offer educational classes. The prisoners began studying English and taking diverse courses, including American history, geography, and civics.

New movies were also added to the camps. The prisoners were allowed to select the film to watch, but given a choice between pre-Nazi German films and the newer American movies, the sophistication of Hollywood nearly always won out. Finally, after American forces had liberated German concentration and POW camps, footage of those hellish places was shown to the German prisoners.

Another important development was the arrival of many German soldiers who had been captured when Allied forces stormed the beaches at Normandy. The success of the American troops in establishing a beachhead on the European continent practically ensured the defeat of Nazi Germany. Prisoners captured after that battle were deliberately spread among all the prison camps to guarantee the news spread. The effect was dramatic. Camp commandants reported that immediately after the influx of new prisoners, violence dropped and the POWs stopped singing the Horst Wessel and other Nazi songs at dinner and during marches to and from work.

Following the surrender of Nazi Germany, the vast majority of the German POWs were shipped to France, forced to rebuild the war-ravaged country before being allowed to return home. However, the U.S. Army decided to reward the prisoners they felt were most favorable to democracy. After completing an intensive, pro-democracy training course, these men were sent directly back to Germany. Candidates would be evaluated by their affiliations to programs that opposed the Nazis, and automatically excluded if they had been part of the SS, Gestapo, or Hitler Youth. Security was extremely light, as the promise of a ticket home kept the men from attempting escape. An intensive, six-day crash course in democracy was prepared, consisting of a film and two lectures, which were followed by open discussions of the lecture topics.

While it is difficult to determine with any precision the effectiveness of a "reeducation program," a poll of the men before they left demonstrates some of the effects of the massive campaign: 96 percent of the men preferred democracy as the form of the next German government, 98 percent did not believe that Germans were the master race, 98 percent would not fight the same war again if given the chance, 99 percent believed that Germans were well suited for democracy, and 90 percent stated that Jews were not to blame for Germany's troubles.

When the remainder of the prisoners were sent back to Europe, almost none of the 10 to 15 percent of hardcore Nazis had been converted. However, estimates show that of the entire POW population, more than 30 percent were definitely anti-Nazi (almost double the incoming estimate) and 60 percent left

America with an increased appreciation of democracy. Many even applied for emigration visas to return to the United States, armed with the ability to speak English and often with job offers from the plants that had employed them during their time as prisoners.

In contrast to the Germans and Japanese, who violated nearly every important rule of the Geneva Convention, the only true, widespread failure of the United States to comply was in delaying the return of the German POWs after the conclusion of the war. The articles of the Convention state, "The repatriation of prisoners shall be effected as soon as possible after the conclusion of peace." Germany formally surrendered on May 8, 1945. However, by the end of 1945, fewer than 75,000 of the 380,000 POWs had been repatriated. The last German prisoner left America's shores by July of 1946, but the vast majority of these prisoners were shipped back to England or France, where they were held for another three years.

Also held in the U.S. prison camps were a group of Russians who had been brought back after the Normandy invasion. The men had been captured by the Germans and forced to work as slave labor on the defenses that protected Normandy, and then captured again by the attacking U.S. forces. The captured Soviets, knowing that their government considered them traitors for working in the service of the enemy, refused to board the trains that would send them home. Many committed suicide rather than waiting to be executed upon their return. American soldiers used tear gas on their own allies to force the remaining Russian prisoners onto a train for San Francisco and the ships that would take them back to the Soviet Union. Relations between America and the USSR were extremely delicate after the surrender of their common enemy, and the Soviet Army still held many American prisoners that they had liberated from German POW camps during the advance toward Berlin. The leadership of the United States decided they couldn't risk the lives of the American prisoners who were still in Soviet hands, and Roosevelt had personally promised Stalin that all citizens of the USSR would be sent home at their meeting at Yalta. So the U.S. government sent the Russian prisoners home, by force, to their deaths. Despite the courage and sacrifice of Papa and the millions of other young men who marched off to war, our nation's greatest victory carried within it a thousand smaller disgraces.

Chapter 11

Coming Home

MY GRANDFATHER LEFT THE HOSPITAL FOUR DAYS LATER, AFTER his "tune-up" had been completed, with a clean bill of health from the doctors. The primary concern was the fluid that had built up in his lungs, which had caused his shortness of breath and exhaustion. The first few days of his hospital stay they tried to treat him with medication. When that failed, the doctors decided that a surgical option was warranted. Snaking a small tube through his ribs and into his lungs, they drained the fluid that had accumulated in the wake of his surgery. More than a liter was removed, and he was released back into my care.

The difference was dramatic. His head was high, not slumped in exhaustion, and some color had returned to his face. Even better, the gurgle had disappeared from his voice and he was breathing freely. He instantly started complaining about his time in the hospital—another good sign.

Even after seeing the transformation, I remained skeptical. After all, the first two days he had been home after his first release had been promising as well. I still didn't know if there was anything I could have done to prevent the downward spiral that sent Papa back to the hospital. Replaying his initial two days in my care, I wondered if I had worn him out, overtaxing him and hurting his recovery. I wasn't going to let history repeat itself. This time we would take things slower.

Papa wanted to immediately began working toward meeting his requirements to go home—before he could leave he had to be able to climb up and down eight stairs and circle the house four times, simulating the climb up his driveway, through his side yard, and into the back door of his house. We started practicing on the stairs the same afternoon he returned from his hospital tune-up, with an enthusiasm I hadn't seen from him since the operation. I limited his attempts to summit the stairs to twice a day, morning and afternoon, during commercial breaks in *The Price Is Right* and *Oprah*. Heaving his body out of the chair with the now-familiar groan of exertion, he would maneuver his walker between the living room chairs, and push his way down the hallway to stand before the staircase—Sisyphus sizing up his mountain.

Standing directly behind him, hands outstretched and gently resting on his lower back for safety, encouragement, and a slight boost, I watched as he hefted the four-legged quad cane. The order of operations was critical to getting him up the stairs. Cane, good leg, bad leg. The knee that Papa had replaced was still weak, and unable to push him up to the next step on its own. Any deviation in the procedure proved disastrous. He would often forget to put the cane up first, resulting in his standing a step above the cane, leaning back to grasp it, and slowly, inevitably, teetering backwards until my hands on his back arrested his fall. Putting the bad leg up first was just as ineffective, though less dangerous. After a few of these catches, I started giving him marching orders, feeling like the sergeant he called me.

"Cane . . . right . . . left. Cane . . . right . . . left."

After each attempt I would pour him a glass of thick strawberry Boost, a high-calorie and high-protein drink the doctor had recommended to help him gain back some of the weight he had lost. The Boost turned his mustache a vibrant pink unknown in nature, which he wouldn't notice until the next time he went to the bathroom—unless I couldn't keep a straight face, in which case we would both burst out laughing.

Day one, he made it up the first two stairs before his strength gave out. Sliding my arm around his back, I supported most of his weight as he turned around on the narrow step and back down. By day two he conquered the six steps up to the landing, where he leaned against the railing, tired and proud and beaming.

I could now easily recognize the symptoms of fatigue: head hanging low, feet shuffling instead of stepping, walker squeaking with stops and starts instead of one continuous motion. Any of these signs sent Papa right back to his chair. When the third day passed without a relapse, I began to slowly let my guard down and enjoy his delight in improving. It was redemptive for me as well, knowing I hadn't been at fault in pushing him too hard earlier—this was how his rehab was supposed to go. It seemed like he gained back more of his strength every hour, walking farther each time he stood. Those nurses and physical therapists who had seen him before all remarked on his dramatic transformation. Color and expression came back into his face, which had been gray and lifeless for so long I had almost forgotten it had ever been another way. His personality, buried under exhaustion, reemerged. Within the week he had ascended the first nine stairs and was already pronouncing himself ready to go home.

With the return of his strength came a renewed interest in our conversations about Stalag IXB. After going through his recovery together, Papa's accounts began to get more personal and intimate. The reserve I had noted in our first interview wasn't gone, but it was certainly reduced. Our discussions now went beyond the facts, and Papa began to open up.

Breathing heavily after an attempt on the stairs, Papa confessed that he had deliberately pushed the experiences from his mind when he returned, desperate to resume his normal life. His repeated, unprompted denial that there was any shame in being captured convinced me of the opposite; for years Papa had been embarrassed by his surrender, that he had destroyed his gun before firing a shot. I realized why the POW conventions were so important to the survivors. The commonality of their experience provided comfort and reassurance that they were not alone, and finally convinced Papa there was nothing to be ashamed of.

As Papa sat in his chair, I perched on the bed a few feet away, hearing for the first time about the nightmares he had from seeing a friend cut in half only a few feet from him. One man in the camp was so traumatized by his experiences that his hair turned from black to gray in a few weeks. Others gave up the hope of rescue that my grandfather clung to in the camp. Papa said they often died a few days later, ostensibly from the cold or disease. I heard more details about how terrible the nights were—shivering as the wind blew through the rips in the tarpaper walls, the fire long since burned out, the combined odor of three hundred unwashed men and the overflowing cesspool at the middle of the barracks making it impossible to breathe, the darkness alive with the groaning, snores, and movements of the other POWs. When he spoke of Charles's death, nearly a decade ago, Papa was fighting back tears.

Just after his return from the "tune-up," Papa told me something about the prison camp, though he could have just as easily been talking about his time in the hospital. "It's a different kind of feeling, when you're in prison. Every right is taken away from you. You have no rights, you just live from one day to the next, and hope you don't die. You do a lot of praying, if you want to get out of there alive. And you never give up hope."

Those days were the most fun that we had together during his entire recovery, despite his constant voicing of a new plan to shave a day—or even a few hours—off his return time. From the first time Papa told us he was ready to go home, it was impossible to trust anything he said. After that moment, according to him, he was never tired, hungry, or in need of anything.

Before sending Papa home, we needed to convince him that he needed help around the house, at least for a little while. When I first mentioned the idea, he immediately retorted that he was fine on his own and I facetiously agreed with him. We sat in silence for a minute or two, until he asked for a glass of water. I've always wanted the ability to raise a single eyebrow, and this would have been the perfect time for it. Instead I just looked at him blankly.

Grumbling, he stood up and crossed the kitchen for his water. He was moving smoothly through getting the glass from the cupboard and filling it at the fridge, but quickly discovered the challenge of keeping a walker bearing true when only using one hand to push, especially when the other is trying not to splash or spill.

After I made my point, I took the glass from his hand and brought it over to his seat. I listed some of the areas where he would struggle living alone: preparing three meals a day in the kitchen, doing laundry, taking his compression socks on and off, running errands. Papa listened, reluctantly, especially to the problem of transportation. The doctor had ordered him to refrain from driving for at least another month, and without a caretaker he wouldn't be able to get groceries or go to the bank. His ability to drive had always been a symbol to him of his independence, and I could tell he was chafing to get back behind the wheel. But until the doctor cleared him, it was the perfect excuse to make him accept a caregiver. After he agreed, we set his return date, several days later.

As soon as he could comfortably climb the stairs, I moved his mattress back upstairs to the guest bedroom. For Papa, it was a challenge more indicative of real life, and one he embraced. He had to scale the stairs at least once a day, and usually a second time for an afternoon nap. With the mattress out of the way, we had a functional living room again, where together we would watch a Laker game or Jeopardy in the evenings.

With him gaining energy daily, we started playing cards at the kitchen table, usually a game called Skip-Bo. My other grandfather, Granddad, also came over a few times, and we played Pinochle together. Papa was more animated, and we would yell together at the contestants on *The Price Is Right*, ridiculing those fools who, for some reason, can't name the price of a Jet Ski or airfare to Mongolia off the top of their heads. He was more mobile, so I started encouraging him to get outdoors for some fresh air. Placing a glass of orange juice and a crossword puzzle on the patio table in the backyard lured him outside each morning, where he could sit for a while. But my best idea, the one I hope makes it into physical therapy textbooks, was Pool Table Therapy.

Papa had taught me to play pool in his basement on a table he saved up for and bought in 1960. He wasn't the greatest teacher. My dad joked that he played by the Fire and Fall Back method, hitting the ball as hard as possible and hoping that something good would happen. Every made shot from Papa was followed by an inevitable lecture about how the game of pool was all about planning and strategy, just like every bad shot was followed by a furious chalking of the pool cue that had let him down.

My father had just bought a pool table of his own, at my urging. It was being sold by a friend down the street, and was where we had wasted most of our summers since junior high. I took Papa out back to shoot some pool with me. He could leave the hated walker behind and cling to the edge of the table for support while I set up the balls, so he wouldn't have to move much to shoot. The first two shots he took missed terribly, but I knew the third one was going in when he bent over farther, tongue protruding between his teeth in his concentration, and buried the eight ball in the corner pocket. He smiled, having done something spontaneous and fun for the first time in months, and I wondered if that was how I had looked the first time I made a shot as he helped me to line it up in his basement. We stayed out for a few more minutes until his legs began to shake with the strain. I brought him back inside and began packing up his clothes for his trip home.

—————

We pulled up to his house, the undercarriage of my car shrieking in familiar protest as it scraped against the concrete of his too-steep driveway, already pitted with scars from similar encounters, announcing his return home to the neighborhood. I yanked my emergency brake as hard as I could, praying it would hold as I opened the trunk to remove his walker and helped him out of the passenger's seat. He was smiling as he started up the driveway, climbing the stairs that would have been unmanageable just a few days earlier, moving just a bit faster than I thought his truncated strength would allow: a triumphal entry suited more for a chariot than a walker, a return home after months of hospital stays and confining, frustrating infirmity. A liberation.

I tried to stay close to him as he climbed up the path to the yard that had proven treacherous the last time we came, but he moved quickly and confidently. As I opened the back door, squeezing aside to let it swing open on the crowded landing, he scooted inside, abandoning his walker for the familiar handholds of his doorjamb and kitchen table as he sat down. My tenuous sergeanthood was stripped as soon as we entered his home, and he began barking orders at his grandson again. Get the mail. Find my checkbook. Start the cars. I brought him his mail, a truly staggering amount dumped through a mail slot in his front door by a long-suffering mailman who had to climb the spiraling brick stairs. The doorbell rang before we could make much of a dent in the pile, and Racquel, the woman who would be his caregiver, came inside.

She was older than I had expected, not a day younger than sixty-five or an inch over five feet tall, with graying hair pulled back into a bun. My first thought was that I hoped Papa had given up on falling into bathtubs, because this woman would need a crane or divine intervention to get him back out. But she had kind eyes and a wonderful lilting South American accent, and my grandfather liked her at once.

The three of us surrounded his small dining room table, talking for a while, making sure he was comfortable with the arrangement and going over what was expected of her: driving when my grandfather went out to run errands, doing some cooking and cleaning, laundry, helping him in and out of the bathtub, and putting his compression socks on in the morning.

I gave her the tour of the rest of the house, showing her the washer and dryer down in the basement and where his car keys were hanging. While we were downstairs and out of Papa's earshot, I let her know about the healing sores on his legs that still needed lotion and that Papa was still a lot weaker than he thought he was. She nodded understandingly, more at my need to make sure he would be fine than at anything I was saying, and we headed back upstairs.

As I was leaving my grandfather began scrambling around, looking for an envelope with my name on it. I knew what was in it; he had been threatening to pay me for nearly a month for taking care of him. I had repeatedly declined out of the embarrassment of discussing money with family, but also because I knew that the amount would be nice, but wouldn't—couldn't—be nearly representative of the time I had spent taking care of him. I had taken the responsibility of his care out of familial duty and necessity, and I didn't want the specter of payment to overshadow that. Defusing the situation for the last time a few weeks prior, I had told him that he could give me something, if he still wanted to, once we got him home. It was my job to get him better, to the point he could live on his own again, and I asked him if he wouldn't think it was odd if a customer paid him for a cabinet halfway through its construction. This answer seemed to satisfy him and, for a time, the topic disappeared from conversation. As I gathered my keys and began to head out the door, he pressed the envelope into my hand as I gave him a handshake, then a hug, congratulating him on his return home and admonishing him to continue his exercises in my absence. By the front door I gently patted his chest. "I told you we'd get you home."

When I got into my car, I rolled down the windows and blasted music the entire way back, elated with getting Papa back to his place, a feeling I knew he shared. For the first time since his surgery, I was free. I could point the car in any direction I chose, stop anywhere I liked, go anywhere I wanted that night. I was free and independent, and, more importantly, so was Papa.

When I got back home it seemed strange, empty and full at the same time. I hadn't realized how accustomed I had become to having my grandfather sitting in his chair or napping in the bed. When I cut up an apple and loaded it with cinnamon and sugar, I wondered why it seemed like I had so many pieces to eat. His side of the dinner table was conspicuously empty and it took several days before my parents and I resumed our normal seats. The house seemed eerily silent without the now-familiar background noises from the living room. No hacking coughs, calls for water, or the telltale squeak of a hospital walker across hardwood floor broke the quiet. For the next several days, it was like living with a ghost. Every time I passed his chair or found something of his lying around to put away, it reminded me of some of the enduring moments of the last few months: celebrating his eighty-ninth birthday and helping him blow out the solitary candle on the cake, the look on his face when he finally summited the stairs, finding him sprawled in the tub with his pants around his ankles and a rolled-up towel behind his head, watching as he tried to eat a sandwich that existed only in his mind, the pink protein shake remnants in his mustache, and, most of all, the notebook on my desk filled with my scrawled account of his time as a prisoner of war. We had learned more about each other in the last three months than in the previous two decades, and I began to miss having him around. Until three o'clock passed without an assault by *Oprah*, which made me freshly grateful I had gotten him back home.

CHAPTER 12

Liberation

*You should have seen how they stormed the camp. The tanks
and armor moved right down the main street and the boys
just went wild. I was so happy to see our troops—tears just
came in my eyes.*

—ROBERT COZEAN, APRIL 2, 1945

*Thank goodness I was only there three and a half months. That
was enough for me—that was a lifetime.*

—ROBERT COZEAN, 2003

THE ATTACK THAT LED TO PAPA'S CAPTURE WAS NAZI GERMANY'S
final offensive of the war. With the Soviets advancing from the
north and the American and British forces driving the German Army from France, Hitler needed something to change
the momentum of the war. He marshaled more than six hundred thousand men across from the advancing American soldiers in the forest of the Ardennes. The goal was to exploit the
overextended Allied line and force a negotiated peace, though
even his own commanders doubted this could be accomplished,
given how depleted the German Army was from the strain of

fighting a war on two fronts. The plan was to attack a concentrated point in the Allies' line of advance, splitting the American and British armies with a lightning thrust. The American army in the Ardennes had eighty thousand men, with four hundred tanks and four hundred artillery weapons, spread across a line nearly eighty miles long. The Germans were able to concentrate more than two hundred thousand men, six hundred tanks, and nineteen hundred artillery pieces across a thin stretch of line—directly across from my grandfather's position.

With the advantage of complete surprise, the German Army charged through the American line under cover of one of the largest artillery barrages in history—the shells that were Papa's introduction to war. Falling back in confusion, two entire regiments were cut off, encircled and captured, the largest surrender of American forces in the war. The German troops were aided by a snowstorm that grounded American airplanes, allowing tanks and supply trucks to move unimpeded by air attack. Driving forward, the German tanks were engaged and slowed by retreating U.S. soldiers, who turned to fight at road junctions and bridges to buy time for the rest of the army to redeploy and meet the attack.

The U.S. retaliation was also hampered by English-speaking German soldiers, dressed in captured American and British uniforms and dog tags stolen from prisoners, who went behind the Allied lines. These infiltrators committed acts of sabotage, giving false directions, changing road signs, and cutting telephone lines. Although security was increased and military checkpoints were set up, it was nearly impossible to tell a real American soldier from an English-speaking German spy. So the security guards resorted to asking questions that only "true Americans" would know, such as the name of Mickey Mouse's girlfriend, who was winning the pennant races in the American and National Leagues, and the names of state capitals. Soldiers who weren't sports fans or who were poor geography students held up progress significantly.

With their forward momentum slowing due to rearguard fighting and ambushes, the German tanks and infantry began encountering increasingly fierce resistance. General Patton and the Third Army, who had been advancing toward the Saar River in Germany, pivoted and plowed into the Germans from the south. As the weather began to clear, American fighters and bombers began to ravage the exposed German columns. In an attempt to stop these attacks, Hitler sent the remainder of the Luftwaffe on a mission to bomb all the Allied airfields they could identify. While the air strike did manage to destroy more than four hundred American planes, the Luftwaffe was crippled in the attack and would not be a factor for the remainder of the war.

Running short of fuel, hammered by airstrikes and confronted with prepared, dug-in troops, the German advance slowed, stopped, and then was reversed as the Allied forces pushed forward across the front. Fierce fighting continued in the Ardennes for more than a month as the American troops regained the lost ground. The German attack, which had relied on surprise and concentrated firepower, was doomed.

The men of my grandfather's regiment were not the only ones to surrender during the initial fighting. On December 17, the same day and not far from where my grandfather was captured, an American company encountered the leading edges of the German assault just outside the city of Malmedy. After a few minutes of fighting, the 113 Americans realized they were hopelessly outnumbered and surrendered. The Germans took all of the men out into a field and gunned them down. Striking the dead and dying with their rifle butts, they fired another bullet into anyone suspecting of surviving. The Malmedy Massacre, as it came to be known, was only one instance where the German forces, desperate to continue advancing, murdered captured soldiers rather than marching them back to a prison camp.

All told, more than one million men fought in the Battle of the Bulge (six hundred thousand German, at least five hundred thousand American, and fifty-five thousand British), the largest American battle of World War II. The American army suffered more than eighty thousand casualties, killed, wounded or captured, while estimates for German casualties range from one hundred thousand to one hundred twenty-five thousand. The defeat broke the military power of the Third Reich and promised a swift defeat of Nazi Germany. The Soviets were sweeping down from the north as America and Britain renewed their push into Germany from the west.

On February 4, 1945, a little more than a week after the conclusion of the Battle of the Bulge and with victory all but assured, three of the most fascinating leaders in history—Prime Minister Winston Churchill, President Franklin D. Roosevelt, and Chairman Joseph Stalin—met in Yalta to determine the shape of postwar Europe. They agreed that nothing but the unconditional surrender of the Nazi regime was acceptable; no deals would be cut with Hitler. After the war, Germany would be split into four occupied zones, controlled by the U.S., Britain, France, and the USSR. This agreement led to the creation of the Berlin Wall and the separation of East and West Germany throughout the Cold War. Churchill pushed hard for democratic elections in Poland, but allowed the USSR to keep the

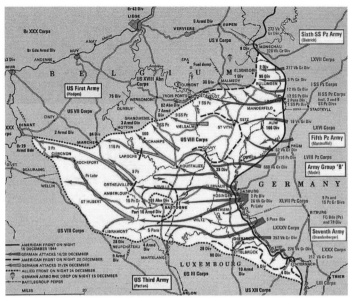

Map of the German attacks during the Battle of the Bulge. My grandfather was part of the 106th Division, on the northern part of the Allied line.

parts of the country they had annexed in 1939. Many members of his own government and, of course, the Polish soldiers who had escaped the German and Russian invasion of their country and returned to fight for the Allies, felt betrayed by the concessions of Churchill and Roosevelt. Stalin would never allow the free election that he had promised. The provisional government the Soviets had installed would eventually oversee a rigged election that turned Poland into a satellite state of the Soviet Union. Stalin also insisted that all Russians in other Allied countries be returned to the Soviets, regardless of their own desires.

Roosevelt elicited a promise that the USSR would declare war on Japan within three months of Germany's surrender. In return, he agreed to recognize Mongolia as a country independent of China, allowing the USSR access to the valuable natural resources there. Though Roosevelt would not live to see it, Japan would surrender within three months of victory in Europe, before the Soviets were obligated to enter the war in the Pacific. Faced with the very real threat of armed conflict with Russia, Churchill and Roosevelt ended up selling both Poland and China down the river in the name of political expediency.

For many captured troops the approaching Allied forces brought danger, rather than rescue. Rumors were flying that the Nazis wouldn't let the prisoners be retaken alive. If they were dead when the American forces arrived, the POWs reasoned, no one would be able to testify against the commandants and guards when the war was over. With the Soviets advancing from the east and the Americans and British from the west, the German High Command began moving their prisoners from the front lines toward the heart of Germany, hoping to hold as many as possible for leverage when negotiating a peace treaty.

With the Russians only five miles away, the German guards evacuated the American POWs at Luft IV prison camp in the middle of a blinding snowstorm. Each prisoner was given a single Red Cross box and the column began marching across Poland, away from the advancing Soviet Army. They covered one hundred miles in the first four days, dragging a wagon filled with both the sick and the dead. Whenever the men passed a cemetery, they would bury their fallen comrades before continuing on. The horse that was drawing the wagon soon died as well, and the prisoners took turns pulling the wagon stacked with their friends. The food quickly ran out, and the prisoners were reduced to trying to trade with the local German civilians or stealing from them. Water was difficult to find and most men survived by eating snow. At night they slept in barns when they could and outside in the fields when there was no shelter available. Pneumonia and dysentery claimed many lives, and some prisoners slipped away from the guards and waited for rescue. Columns that began with two thousand men concluded with fewer than three hundred. All told, the prisoners of Luft IV covered over six hundred miles over the course of eighty-seven days on their death march, most of it without food, water, or shelter. There is no accurate count of how many American POWs were killed in the final days of the war, with rescue only a few miles away.

In late March the American forces approached Stalag XII-A, just a few miles west of the camp that still housed my grandfather. The POWs there were forced onto a train bound for Berlin. Before leaving the prison camp, they spent thirty-six hours locked in the boxcars without any food, relieving themselves in a pile of straw in the corner, the air rapidly becoming unbearable. Once it finally began moving, the boxcar, bereft of any markings that would indicate prisoners were aboard, was spotted by American pilots. The planes began firing on the train, which sought refuge inside a tunnel. The engineer waited, with the men still trapped, another day and a half within the tunnel before emerging. Again the train was strafed by American fighter planes, which blew up a railroad car. Desperately a group of prisoners pried open the barbed wire that covered the window of the boxcar and slithered through, slicing their skin and falling to the ground below. With their friends still trapped in the boxcar, the escaped POWs needed a way to signal to the planes. Sprinting into the field beside the train tracks they stripped off their shirts and spelled out "P-O-W" with their bodies on the ground. After what seemed like an eternity the planes pulled up from their strafing run. The escapees were recaptured soon after and would have to wait several more weeks to be rescued.

At Stalag IXB, the first hint of freedom was heard two weeks before the prison camp was liberated. One prisoner, a former field artillery man, swore that he recognized American mortars firing in the distance. On March 26 Papa, always optimistic, wrote in his diary, "Pea soup, news is good," but he had reported the same "good news" in his diary on February 2, January 22, and January 6—ten days after entering the camp. Most of the other prisoners wouldn't believe the hopeful rumors until they saw with their own eyes the tanks with the U.S. Army emblem entering the compound. Many thought they would be shot or moved by the camp authorities before American forces could arrive.

With the men of Patton's command only a few miles away, the camp commandant had ordered the fifteen hundred men to begin walking east, away from rescue. The Red Cross representative was extremely concerned about the possibility that the camp would be evacuated after his visit:

> *The consequences of a new evacuation of these camps are barely conceivable. Much of the prisoners could not endure a simply walk or any exercise. There is more special attention devoted to Stalag neighboring the front, which may be evacuated first. In the "Wegrkreis" IX, these are the Stalag IX A and Stalag IX B.*

The leader of the POWs protested the planned evacuation, saying the men would never survive a forced march in their weakened state. When the commandant insisted, the new Man of Confidence went to the camp's medical officer, who had demonstrated his utter apathy toward the suffering of the prisoners, and reported that the men might be infected with typhoid. Moving them, he argued, created the possibility of a typhoid epidemic among the local population. The medical officer didn't bother to examine the men, but imposed a ten-day quarantine to keep the disease confined within the camp—saving the men from a death march.

When the Army arrived, those who were able stood outside and cheered. It was Easter morning, April 1, 1945. The men had entered Stalag IXB just after Christmas and were freed on Easter, a fact that my grandfather, a lifelong Presbyterian, never mistook for coincidence.

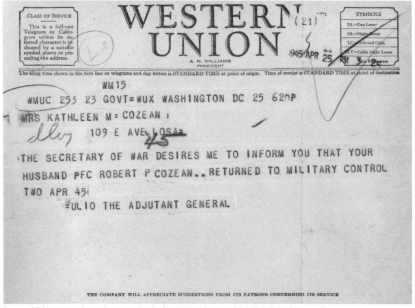

It would be more than three weeks before Kitty learned her husband was safe.

As the emaciated prisoners emerged from the barracks to greet their liberators, the troops tossed down boxes of rations. But after months of thin soup and scraps of bread, the former captives were unable to hold anything down. It took less than two minutes for the starved prisoners to begin vomiting. The incoming troops were more focused on driving back the retreating German Army than dealing with rescued prisoners, so the POWs, now free, were left in the same barracks where they had spent the last four months. They couldn't even eat the food that had been left behind, so their diets remained the same—bread and soup— although they could finally eat all that their shrunken stomachs could hold. The POWs, now survivors, shattered the lock on the storeroom and took over the kitchen, cooking a thick potato soup for themselves.

His stomach full for the first time in months, my grandfather took advantage of the broken-down front gates and walked across the street to a bar that had been abandoned by the locals when the Allied forces closed in. The prisoners had stared at it through the barbed wire during the bleak winter months, just across the street but as distant as home. A souvenir shot glass from that bar became a prized possession, displayed on a countertop in his house.

Continuing his first stroll as a free man on legs unsteady from months of starvation, he entered an empty German home, searching for something he had been denied throughout his captivity, and he found it. That night, Papa's first night of freedom, was spent back in his prison barracks, still filthy, still emaciated, still riddled with lice, and still sleeping on wooden planks—but enfolded between two clean sheets with a pillow under his head.

The date of my grandfather's liberation, April 1, 1945, is a day that is critical in the history of my family, surrounded by the days

Rescue comes too late for 33 Americans

(By United Press)

Thirty-three American prisoners, incredibly emaciated and filthy, died of malnutrition yesterday just a few minutes after the 106th cavalry group of the Seventh United States army liberated them from a German prison camp at Bad Orb, radio correspondent Seymour Korman reported.

Korman said 6500 men were held in a camp designed for 1500 and that all of them were on the verge of starvation.

The prisoners included 3200 Americans captured in the Ardennes salient last December, 2200 British, including veterans of Dunkirk imprisoned since 1940. The rest were Serbs, Russians and French.

The prisoners reported they were brought to the camp after marching 36 hours without food, and that they marched 146 miles through snow. Nazi guards beat stragglers with rifle butts, Korman said.

Newspaper article written about the liberation of Papa's camp that he saved and brought home; a reminder of how lucky he had been to survive.

that are remembered in history books. It was 1,207 days after the United States declared war on Germany and 103 days after he had staggered through the gates of Stalag IXB. It was only ten days before Franklin D. Roosevelt died of a cerebral hemorrhage and Harry Truman ascended to the presidency to oversee the end of World War II, twenty-seven days before Benito Mussolini, Hitler's closest ally, was murdered as he tried to flee Italy, twenty-nine days before Hitler put a well-deserved bullet through his brain in the depths of his bunker, and thirty-seven days before the Allies declared victory in Europe on May 8, 1945.

Finally given a pencil and paper, my grandfather quickly put them to use, writing to his wife on the same day that the camp was liberated:

April 2, 1945
Dearest Kitty:
Well sweets, today I am a free man and I am sure happy too.
Now I know I am going to see you soon. They told us we would
be home in the states in a month . . . You should have seen
how they stormed the camp. The tanks and armor moved right
down the main street and the boys just went wild. I was so
happy to see our troops—tears just came in my eyes. I couldn't
write you every day of capture but I will as much as I can now
. . . I can say tonight that I can feel more for the first time in
months, sweets. I can't begin to tell you how happy I am and I
know now I will see you soon. I am going to write you every
day and I miss you so. And I just can't wait to see you. Well,
honey, I will close for tonight and I love you more and more.
A million kisses to you.
Lots of Love, Bob

April 3, 1945
Dearest Kitty:
Well sweets are still at the camp but the GP (jeep) moved in
today and brought C-Rations so we are to have American
food now and it really tasted good and I am full to the top
now . . . Three meals a day too. We got the shops and shipment
too dated yesterday so I read the paper over and over again.
It was so good to read the news that I read it over and over
again . . .
Lots of Love, Bob

The U.S. Army returned as promised, three days after they first reached the camp, ready to deal with the liberated prisoners. Red Cross boxes of food found stacked from floor to ceiling in the German quarters of the camp were distributed to the men. My grandfather's diary for that day records, "Got Red Cross box, part coffee, donuts." The men were stripped of lice, their constant torment in captivity, by a delousing powder, sprayed in their faces and up and down their backs. With the lice gone and fresh uniforms draped over their shrunken frames, the emancipated prisoners were finally taken to a hospital, where most of them spent the night. Some of the men were so starved and weak they could hardly stand. The doctor looked at my grandfather, little more than a flesh-covered skeleton after losing sixty pounds, shook his head, and merely told him to try and gain a little weight back. My grandfather remembered, "As long as you were walking, I guess you were all right."

Later that night, well after the hospital kitchen had been closed, my grandfather ran into a captain, who asked how he was doing. He told the officer he was doing as well as could be expected, but that he was craving some hot cocoa. The captain himself went down to the kitchen to make my grandfather a cup of hot chocolate. The memory of this simple act of kindness stuck with Papa for more than sixty years, and joined with a regret that he didn't get the name of the benevolent officer. It was a simple act of kindness that meant everything to a man deprived of human decency for too long.

The familiar Army routine of hurry up and wait was restored, with the men still stuck in camp a week after liberation. Papa's frustration with sitting still instead of heading home is apparent in his letter to Kitty.

April 5, 1945
Dearest Kitty:
Well sweets this is the close of another day and we are still in
Camp. We couldn't get on the planes so we are here another
day. Red Cross came in with coffee and donuts and we were
able to write a letter today so you should get it from me in
about 10 days and I hope by that time I am a lot closer to home
and I can't get on the way too soon . . . So the days are slowly
passing by and each day leaving one closer to you. I am slowly
getting weight back on. Three meals a day are a lot better than
one like we used to get. I have a lot of things to tell you sweets.
I just can't seem to wait to see you and it has been such a long
time.

Well sweets, I will close for now. A million kisses to you—
pleasant dreams and I love you.
Lots of Love, Bob

My grandfather and the other rescued prisoners waited at the hospital for trucks to drive them to Camp Lucky Strike at Le Havre, on the coast of France. Then an officer thought to send them back on the empty gasoline planes that had just landed to fuel Patton's drive to Berlin. The men were grateful for their rapid return, even though my grandfather remembered sitting on his own hands during the flight because his "ass-bone was sticking right through." That was the first time my grandfather or any of the men he knew had ever been on an airplane.

At the camp at Le Havre the next morning, breakfast was served at 6:00, 8:00, and 10:00 a.m. After the last opportunity for breakfast, the commandant strolled out to announce, "We have two hundred men at this camp, but we just served six hundred breakfasts. Where do you think they all came from?" The men just grinned guiltily at each other—their stomachs had shrunk so dramatically that they were unable to hold down more than a few bites of solid food at a time, and so they continued to pour through the chow lines at every opportunity, slowly gaining back weight and strength.

At Lucky Strike, the camp surgeon posted a warning to freed prisoners regarding their health, stating:

Take the Doctor's Advice:

The Medical Department welcomes you—You have just been liberated from your enemy, the Germans. It is up to you now to liberate yourselves from your new enemy—your appetite and your digestive system.

After eating here several times, you may begin to wonder what the score is, why the medics won't let you gorge yourself with doughnuts and hotdogs complete with mustard and sauerkraut, about which you must have dreamed for months. You may begin to wonder why the mess supervisors won't let you come back for seconds when you are still hungry. There's a reason for it!

Most of you have been on a starvation diet for months. A regular diet consisting of coarse German bread and watery soup when taken over a period of weeks and months does something to your stomach, digestive system, and entire body. You have lost tremendous weight; there have been changes in your digestive system, your skin, and other organs. You have become weak and are susceptible to diseases. You almost all have the GI's.

The reason is that you lack vitamins and you have lost the proteins so necessary in building healthy, solid tissues and muscles. The lining of your stomach is sore, delicate, inflamed, and irritated. Your stomach has shrunk. If you overload that weak, small, sore stomach of yours, you will become acutely ill. Your belly will become swollen and painful. You will have cramps and your diarrhea will be much worse. Some of you will have to be hospitalized and even become very seriously ill.

You must overcome this terrible craving of yours and curb your appetites. You must realize that to become well quickly and get back to normal you must eat small feedings at frequent intervals until gradually you can once again tolerate a normal diet.

The food you will be served is good and you will get more than enough. If you get hungry between meals go to the Red Cross for cocoa and eggnog. Just don't drink too much. The first kitchen you will go to will feed you a soft, bland, non-irritating diet. Your next kitchen will give you a diet which approaches normal. Know this is for your own good.

The Medical Department advises you to obey the following rules and build yourselves gradually to the point where you can once again eat anything you want and as much as you want, without getting severely ill.

Eat only as much as you are given in the chow line.

Don't come back for seconds.

Take the vitamin pills that are given to you in the mess line (and swallow them).

Go to the Red Cross for eggnog or cocoa between meals if you get hungry. Don't drink more than one cup.

Don't overeat. If you overload your small stomach, you will get sick.

Don't eat candy, peanuts, doughnuts, frankfurters, pork, rich gravies, liquor, spicy foods, or anything that you know will make you sick.

There are three dispensaries in each of the three areas where you will bivouac. As you move from one area to the other, go to the dispensary in that area. Sick call will be held between 0800-1700 hours. After that, come only for an emergency.

The men obeyed and gradually began to regain their strength, although it would take them months to gain back the weight they had lost as guests of the Germans.

While waiting for transportation home, a much funnier bulletin was posted and saved by my grandfather. I found it later, among his letters, a three page, typewritten copy on something resembling tissue paper. I'm not sure whether it was authorized by the camp management or whether it was something written by a former prisoner with access to a typewriter, but it showed the sense of humor that had survived their ordeals.

Subject: Indoctrination for Return to U.S.
To: All Units

In compliance with current policies for rotation of armed forces overseas, it is directed that, in order to maintain the high standard of character of the American Soldier and to prevent any dishonor to reflect on the uniform, all individuals eligible for return to the U.S. under current directives will undergo an indoctrination course of Demilitarization prior to approval of his application for return.

The following points will be emphasized in the subject indoctrination course:

In America there is a remarkable number of beautiful girls. These young girls have not been liberated and many are gainfully employed as stenographers, sales girls and beauty operators or welders. Contrary to current practices, they should not be approached with "How much." A proper greeting is "Isn't it a lovely day?" or "Have you ever been to Chicago?" Then say, "HOW MUCH?"

A guest in a private home is usually awakened in the morning by a light tapping on his door and an invitation to join the host at breakfast. It is proper to say "I'll be there shortly." Do not say, "BLOW IT OUT YOUR __."

A typical American breakfast consists of such strange foods as cantaloupes, fresh eggs, milk, ham, etc. These are highly palatable and though strange in appearance, are extremely tasty. Butter, made from cream, is often served. If you wish some butter, you turn to the person nearest you and say quietly, "Please pass the butter." You do not say "THROW ME THE GODDAM GREASE."

Very natural urges are apt to occur when in a crowd. If found necessary to defecate, one does not grab a shovel in one hand and paper in the other and run for the garden. At least 90% of American homes have one room called the BATHROOM, i.e., a room that, in most cases contains a bathtub, wash basin, medicine cabinet, and a toilet. It is the latter that you will use in this case. Instructors should make sure that all personnel understand the operation of a toilet, particularly the lever or button arrangement that serves to prepare the device for re-use.

In the event a helmet is retained by the individuals, they will refrain from using it as a chair, wash bowl, foot-bath or bathtub. All these devices are furnished in the average American home. It is not considered good practice to squat Indian fashion in a corner in the event all chairs are occupied. The host will usually furnish suitable seats.

Belching or passing wind in company is strictly frowned upon. If you should forget about it, however, and belch in the presence of others, a proper remark is "Excuse me." Do not say, "IT MUST BE THE LOUSY CHOW WE HAVE BEEN GETTING."

American dinners, in most cases, consist of several items, each served in a separate dish. The common practice of mixing various items, such as corned beef and pudding, or lima beans and peaches, to make it more palatable will be refrained from. In time the "separate dish" system will become very enjoyable.

Americans have a strange taste for stimulants. The drinks in common usage on the European continent, such as under ripe wine, alcohol and grapefruit juice, or gasoline bitters and water (commonly known by the French term "Cognac") are not ordinarily acceptable in civilian circles. These drinks should be served only to those who are definitely not within the inner circle of friends. A suitable use for such drinks is for serving to one's landlord in order to break an undesirable lease.

The returning soldier is apt to often find his opinions differ from those of his civilian associates. One should call upon his reserve etiquette and correct his acquaintance with such remarks as "I believe you have made a mistake," or "I'm afraid you are in error on that." Do not say "BROTHER, YOU'VE REALLY F___D UP." This is considered impolite.

Upon leaving a friend's home after a visit, one may find his hat misplaced. Frequently it has been placed in a closet. One should turn to one's host and say "I don't seem to have my hat. Could you help me find it?" Do not say, "DON'T ANY-BODY LEAVE THIS ROOM. SOME SON OF A B____ HAS STOLEN MY HAT!"

In travelling in the U.S. particularly in a strange city, it is often necessary to spend the night. Hotels are provided for this purpose and one can get directions to the nearest hotel from anyone. Here for a small sum one can register and be shown a room where he can sleep for the night. The present practice of entering the nearest house, throwing the occupants into the yard, and taking over the premises will cease.

Whiskey, a common American drink, may be offered to the soldier on social occasions. It is considered a reflection on the uniform to snatch the bottle from the hostess and drain the bottle, cork and all. All individuals are cautioned to exercise extreme control in these circumstances.

In motion picture theaters, seats are provided. Helmets are not required. It is not considered good form to whistle every time a female over 8 and under 80 crosses the screen. If vision is impaired by the person in the seat in front, there are plenty of other seats which can be occupied. Do not hit him across the back of the head and say "MOVE YOUR HEAD, JERK, I CAN'T SEE A DAMN THING."

It is not proper to go around hitting everyone of draft age in civilian clothes. He might have been released from the service for medical reasons. Ask him for his credentials, and if he can't show them, then go ahead and slug him.

Upon retiring, one will often find a pair of pajamas laid out on the bed. (Pajamas, it should be explained, are two-piece garments which are donned after all clothing has been removed.) The soldier confronted with these garments should assume an air of familiarity and act as though he were used to them. A casual remark such as, "Isn't it a delicate shade of blue" will usually suffice. Under no circumstances say, "WHO IN THE HELL DO YOU EXPECT TO SLEEP IN A GET-UP LIKE THIS?"

Natural functions will continue. It may be necessary frequently to urinate. Do not walk behind the nearest tree or automobile you find to accomplish this. Toilets (1D above) are provided in all public buildings for this purpose. Signs on some will read LADIES which literally means, "OFF LIMITS TO ALL TROOPS."

Beer is sometimes served in bottles. A cap remover is usually available and it is not good form to open a bottle by the use of one's teeth.

Air raids and enemy patrols are not encountered in America. Therefore, it is not necessary to wear the helmet to church, or at social gatherings or to hold weapon at ready, loaded and cocked, when talking to civilians in the street.

Every American home and all hotels are equipped with bathing facilities. When desired to take a bath, it is not considered good form to find the nearest pool or stream, strip down and indulge in a bath. This particularly is true in heavily populated areas.

All individuals returning to the U.S. will make effort to conform to the customs and habits of the regions visited and to make themselves as inconspicuous as possible. Any actions which reflect on the honor of the uniform will be promptly dealt with.

Picture that Papa had taken when on leave in Paris.

A week after being liberated, the men lingered in Europe, awaiting transport home. The commanding officer of the base offered a four-day pass to any former prisoner who was physically able and willing to take it while they waited to go home. Having regained some of his strength, Papa eagerly accepted and set off to see Paris.

There was my grandfather, twenty-four years old, freed from a German prison camp and seeing Paris like millions of young men before and since. But unlike most, he wasn't celebrating his college graduation with a summer of backpacking in Europe, or his wedding with a romantic honeymoon—he was celebrating his release, his liberty, and the restoration of his life.

He and his friends paid a cabbie ten American dollars to show them the whole of Paris. They climbed to the top of L'Arc de Triomphe (given new meaning by the French Resistance and the recapture of Paris) and halfway up the Eiffel Tower, and found time to purchase a few "French Postcards," which are evidently too racy for his grandson to see. They went past Notre Dame, walked the Champs-Élysées, ate at fancy French restaurants they could never have afforded before the war, and saw a play. Staying at the U.S.O., they could buy a carton of cigarettes for fifty cents and trade them for anything they wanted while in the city. American cigarettes—Lucky Strikes, Camels, Chesterfields—were like gold. Or potatoes.

CHAPTER 13

Robert Cozean Released, Now Enroute Home

I WISH, MORE THAN ANYTHING, THAT I COULD WRITE A HAPPY ending to this story, that I could report Papa had cheated death once again. I would love to finish the final chapter with him taking the motorcycle ride that he wanted for his ninetieth birthday off into the sunset. But this time his liberation from pain and suffering was accomplished not by tanks and generals, but by a peaceful passing in the bedroom of the house he had built with his own hands sixty-three years before. I woke suddenly that morning, well before the dawn or any alarm, with a sense of foreboding. Later I discovered my father experienced the same feeling. Neither of us could go back to sleep, and neither of us was surprised when Racquel found him in his bedroom when she came into work that morning.

The day before he had taken a turn for the worse and had been struggling to breathe. Racquel wanted to take him to the hospital, but Papa stubbornly refused. The most he would allow was a visit by one of the home health nurses. After examining him, the nurse said that she was concerned by his breathing, but thought he was safe for the night, and recommended that he see his cardiologist the next day. We were all worried, but nothing was going to convince Papa to head back to the hospital.

I had last seen him only three days before, New Year's Day, and he looked stronger and happier than any time since his surgery. Papa's house is walking distance from the Rose Parade, and my parents had grown up heading down to see the flower-covered floats every year on January 1st. The year before we took visiting friends from Kenya, camping out on the parade route for our spots and stopping by Papa's afterward to shower and change. Nicole and I had returned to the Rose Parade, and we stopped by to visit him. He was excited to see us, throwing open his thick front door and beaming as we entered. I dropped off some food for him in the kitchen, and he asked me to go and start his cars to keep the batteries charged. He was supposed to be using his walker, but usually just steadied himself with a hand against the wall. We spent a little more than an hour talking in his kitchen, hearing about how he and Racquel were getting along and his plans for the next few weeks. He was already looking forward to a February trip to Palm Springs with the Girls, hopeful he would be strong enough. Seeing him sitting upright at his kitchen table, smiling and laughing, I certainly wasn't betting against him. I helped him put on his compression socks one more time before we left.

As Nicole and I were about to leave, he asked if I could drive him over to visit Pat, saving her the trip to pick him up. I helped him down the now-familiar perils of his steep driveway, folded his walker into the trunk, and supported his weight as he slid into the front seat. We arrived at Pat's apartment, and I let him out of the car. Driving away, I saw Papa for the last time in the rearview mirror, a big smile on his face, one hand on the walker and the other waving goodbye.

⌒

The following week was consumed with notifying his friends and family, making funeral arrangements, and planning his memorial service. In the midst of it I was able to spend a few quiet hours alone at his house, going through old photo albums to find pictures for his service. I had never been alone there before. Nothing had been moved; it was all how I had last seen it, cluttered and cozy and still slightly musty. It was as if he had never left. I talked aloud, at first only to break the silence of his home, but the words began pouring out. I told Papa how disappointed I was with the way things had turned out, that I wished we could have gotten him back to full strength. I told him how grateful I was that I had been able to spend the last few months with him, first interviewing him about his experiences in the war before his surgery and then taking care of him until he was able to return home.

On his nightstand in a plain manila envelope was the first draft of his story, which I had given to him at Christmas, less than two weeks before and almost sixty-five years to the day after he entered the prison camp at Stalag IXB. I had driven him home after our family Christmas dinner and, in hindsight, our conversation about Christmas cards seems prophetic.

Christmas cards are the way that many of the former prisoners communicate with each other and slowly, inexorably, the cards are drying up. On the drive back to his house, Papa mentioned a few men he had known in the camp. Three years earlier he had called the sergeant in command of his company on a Sunday afternoon, only to find that his friend was barely able to talk—his wife had passed away that Friday. That was the last time Papa heard from him; he hadn't received a call or card since. Another Christmas card from an old friend was missing that year, and Papa was hoping he was just late with sending them out. These men, all survivors, were gradually fading away, their stories evaporating with them. The thick folder I placed in his hands on that drive, and later retrieved from the nightstand, contained my promise to Papa that his experience wouldn't suffer the same fate.

A few days after he passed away the phone rang, and I recognized Racquel's lilting voice immediately. She soon broke down sobbing, apologizing, blaming herself for Papa's refusal to go to the hospital. It was heartbreaking to hear her cry, and my eyes filled with tears. When I entered Papa's house alone, it hit me that he was really gone, but hearing a stranger grieving over the phone pounded his absence home.

I wrote her a letter after she hung up, convinced I would never see her again.

Dear Racquel,

I wanted to thank you for the work you did taking care of my grandfather in the last month. It was very important to him to be able to live at home, and you were the reason he was able to do that. While he was down here recovering with us he kept making excuses to try and get home earlier. We came up and spent one night before he had to go to a doctor's appointment, and he was so happy to be home, in his own bed, even for just one night. My family and I are so grateful that he was able to spend his last days at home, and grateful to you for allowing him to stay there and be in the home he loved. He spoke very highly of you and the job you were doing, and I know that he enjoyed your company greatly.

I know that we all have a tendency to blame ourselves for what happened. That night, I had a bad feeling and almost drove up to see him and spend the night, but I talked myself out of it. Ever since I heard the news I have been wondering if I would have been able to help him if I had come up. I woke up at 4:00 that morning, wide awake, with a feeling of profound sadness. I'm sure it must be just as difficult for you, especially being the one who had to find him. But I want you to know that my family and I know that you took great care of him, and there was nothing that any of us could have done. He had his alert bracelet on, so he should have been able to trigger the alarm if he realized there was a problem. His heart may have just finally given out.

Please don't blame yourself for anything that happened. You were the person who allowed him to spend his final days in the home that he had built, where he had lived for almost 50 years, where he had loved and lost his wife, and where he had raised his family. If it wasn't for you and your help, we would have had to move him into a nursing facility, and he would have hated that. You brightened up the last days of his life, and I will be forever grateful.

Sincerely,

Jesse Cozean

When my parents and I began the emotional process of going through Papa's belongings, we tried to figure out why he wasted money on trash pickup all those years. I don't think any of us, even my dad, had realized the extent and volume of the stuff Papa had collected. Tucked away in the basement was an unused relic of a washer, filled to the brim with old coins. Every pay stub

185

Papa had ever earned was tossed into a shoebox and preserved in a closet. Four separate toolboxes, filled with rusting tools made by companies long since out of business, littered the woodshop. And every piece of clothing had to be checked individually—we found almost $7,000 in cash scattered in pockets and other hiding places.

The piano that decorated the living room was a baby grand with stiff keys, bought in 1960. When I crawled under and saw the inscribed date, we realized that it must have been the result of a deal cut between Papa and his wife—he got a pool table when she got a piano. It certainly wasn't worth the cost of moving, so we agreed to sell it and put the proceeds back into the estate. Unfortunately, it wouldn't sell for $800, or $400. We were worried we would have to pay movers to take it out of the house when we caught a break. A group of men with matching uniforms and a moving truck came by. They entered the house and carried the piano down the front steps, even stopping to talk with Ray for a few minutes. Of course, none of us had called any movers; I just hope the thieves had more luck selling it than we did.

The most exciting moment of the day was when my dad found a pistol in a workshop drawer and, before handing it to me, managed to both remove the clip and cock it. Suddenly I'm holding a World War I vintage handgun, which is ready to fire, and my dad and I are left debating, from our experiences with TV dramas, whether there can still be a bullet in the chamber after the clip is removed. In retrospect, there must be a way to un-cock (de-cock?) a gun, but I still don't know how to do it. If Papa was watching, the Army weapons specialist, he must have been rolling on the floor laughing at my dad and me, wondering how he failed us so badly. I finally pointed the gun at a big pile of scrapwood, where I thought it would cause the least amount of damage, and pulled the trigger. Fortunately Papa must have known that no one else in his family should ever be trusted with a loaded gun, because all I heard was a click as the hammer fell.

My dad proved he was truly his father's son as we went through Papa's belongings. Anything that he could carry ended up leaving with us. That's how I ended up walking backwards down Papa's steep brick stairs underneath a three hundred pound electronic organ. Three van loads later, my dad had filled his guest bedroom with stuff from Papa's house.

After the estate sale, we went back through what was left, determining what should be thrown out and what could be given away. Toward the end of the day I was on a stepladder, going through shelves built into the wall above Papa's bedroom closet. They were filled with empty boxes, the kind that clothes or hats come in. I must have pulled out fifty of them, some loose, some stacked inside each other. I don't know what he kept the boxes for—certainly not for presents. Papa had figured out that cash was the best present for a grandson long before the rest of my family. Every birthday and Christmas a crisp $50 bill could be found among the ill-fitting sweaters and ponderous presidential biographies, and he would grin when I asked him how he always knew exactly what I wanted.

Standing on top of the ladder, I reached into the very back of the shelf, pulling out the only box that had any weight to it. Opening it, I uncovered the ossified remains of the top layer of a wedding cake, complete with the bride and groom figurines on top. Even for Papa, this was unbelievable—he had saved the top of his wedding cake for sixty-nine years. As I tried to hand it down to my mother, I felt it slide within the box and shift the balance right out of my hand. I watched helplessly as it tumbled down, the bride and groom lying on a pile of rubble on the floor of Papa's bedroom.

—◆—

Most of the funeral was just a blur. I remember the laughter at the photo in the slideshow I put together that featured Papa in the Harley-Davidson museum in Vegas, wearing an American flag headband, on a huge motorcycle, with both the Girls hanging on the back. The most emotional moment came with the playing of "Taps" by the Army, looking around the room to see every man over eighty standing as tall and proud as age would allow, saluting as the flag was folded and presented to my father. I don't believe any other generation will ever be as united by struggle and sacrifice as that of my grandfather.

When the pastor asked if anyone wanted to share a memory, one man in the back of the room stood up. He introduced himself as the son of the owner of the cabinetry shop where my grandfather had worked for so many years and reflected on what Papa had meant to the business and the people who worked there. Surrounding him were other men from the shop, many of whom Papa had trained when they were just starting out. In talking to him afterward, I learned that Papa had continued to visit the shop regularly, usually about once a month, to check in with everyone and update them on his travels. One time he brought in the Bronze Star he had been awarded for his service. Papa had even told them about being interviewed by me. He had given many of them their first jobs, trained them, and kept in touch more than twenty years after he retired. It was a side of Papa I hadn't seen before—the exacting craftsman, the patient teacher, the boss. He had retired before I was born, and yet the men he worked with still cared enough to postpone their work to listen to his stories and come to show their support at his funeral. It amazed me, even after all the time we had spent together, how much I still didn't know about Papa.

I did end up seeing Racquel again at Papa's memorial service. I gave her the most sincere hug that someone who is 6'3" can give someone her size. She reminds me of the captain at Camp Lucky Strike who snuck into the kitchen to bring Papa the cup of hot cocoa. The unexpected kindness stuck with Papa for years. It was one of the least important of the stories he told, but the most meaningful to him.

Papa had told his pastor, like everyone else, that he was a POW survivor. The only thing I remember from the pastor's address at the funeral was, "He was a survivor—right up until the day he died." I almost laughed aloud at the unintentional comedy in that statement. After all, you could say the same thing at any funeral, whether it was for someone who was twenty-two or eighty-nine. But it resonated, and I realized that it did perfectly state the reason his death had blindsided me. Although I had seen his body betray him, I had continued to believe that my grandfather would be around for a long time to come.

A phrase was running through my mind, distracting and unbidden, during the funeral and the small talk afterward. It was the title of a newspaper story written by the local paper when my grandfather was liberated, sixty-five years ago. It was preserved as a clipping in the binder of documents that Papa had saved, and I had scanned it and included it in the copy of his story I had given him on our last Christmas together:

Robert Cozean Released, Now Enroute Home.

Epilogue

ONE STORY OF PAPA'S STRUCK ME WHEN I HEARD IT THAT FIRST Thanksgiving night, and it means even more to me now, nearly a year and a half after his death. Upon entering the prison camp, and at gunpoint, the men were ordered to empty all valuables into a helmet, like a collection plate being passed around at church—money, watches, and jewelry. After emptying his wallet, Papa slipped it back into his pocket, where it remained throughout his four months in Stalag IXB. It contained his driver's license and pictures of his family, his only reminder of civilian life and the wife he had waiting back home. Everything else was either supplied by the U.S. Army, like the solitary uniform he wore throughout his imprisonment, or by the Germans.

After the camp was liberated, Papa received a fresh uniform, and the wallet was transferred to a new pocket. It had travelled across the Atlantic Ocean in a troopship, been carried into the Battle of the Bulge, seen the surrender of the American troops and the long march into captivity down the road as German tanks rattled past, been crammed with sixty other men into a boxcar, taken deep into the heart of Nazi Germany, spent four months in the biting cold of the prison camp, and celebrated freedom with a four-day pass to Paris. He was sitting on it on the troopship, heading home, when the announcement came that Germany had surrendered. The wallet was tattered and torn, battered by the same captivity my grandfather had experienced, but it had endured—until it was stolen from under my grandfather's pillow by a member of the U.S. Army on the ship home.

For me, this story was more powerful than the accounts of his capture, the boxcar ride into Germany, standing at attention in a driving snowstorm, the casket with the trapdoor, even his friend being cut in half by friendly fire. It was the story I wrote down first when I headed upstairs after he went to bed that Thanksgiving night. It was a reminder of how stunning our ignorance of other people is. The person who stole the wallet had no idea of what it meant to Papa; it had been his only link home for four months, when he was wondering if he would ever see the family in his photographs again. And it made me wonder if my grandfather ever felt like that wallet. After surviving the German prison camp, he came home to his wife, family, and friends. Everything had changed, but everything stayed the same when he returned. No one could hope to comprehend what he had gone through, and for more than half a century Papa kept his story hidden away. How often did people look at him over those four decades and just see something plain, ordinary? Just a carpenter, just a boss, just a customer in a restaurant, just a husband, just a kindly old grandfather.

Time has passed, as it tends to do, and the pain of losing Papa is fading. It's hard to see tragedy in the death of someone who is nearly ninety years old. As Granddad—my sole remaining grandparent—told me at the funeral when he saw me fighting back tears, "He lived a good long life and helped a lot of people. What's there to be sad about?" His words were a simple eulogy that brought no comfort at the time, but one that I know Papa would agree with.

Despite all the time we spent together in his final months, it was only after Papa's death that I truly began to understand him. Only a few weeks after the funeral, my search for a house of my own was satisfied when I purchased a run-down place in San Clemente, whose best feature was its proximity to the beach. I wish I would have been able to show it to him. I could have used Papa's advice as I fixed it up: tearing out the hideous, inch-thick black tile and covering the floor with hardwood, ripping out and replacing the carpet, repainting both inside and out, rebuilding the rotted-out walkway up to my front door. It only took a year and a half of backbreaking labor before I began to understand why Papa's home was so important to him. I can't imagine how much more attached he was to the place he built up from the foundation and raised a family in.

Several pieces of furniture fashioned by my grandfather are now in my new home. Every morning I eat my bowl of Wheaties at the same table where I first interviewed him. The nightstand by my bed served in his guest bedroom for decades. My clothes rest in a cedar chest that he built and I restored. And his pool table, where he taught me how to play, has been refelted and refurbished and now occupies my living room.

I have also undergone a surgery of my own, though as far removed—both in anatomical distance and severity—from Papa's procedure as possible. My ankle, after years of abuse on the basketball court, decided to abruptly retire. Watching over Papa taught me how hard it is to take care of someone else; my own surgery showed me how much strength it took for Papa to let himself be taken care of. In the family tradition, I stayed in my parents' living room for the week after surgery. Once again, my dad was in his element—driving down to the store three times a day to pick up fruit smoothies (the only thing my narcotic-induced nausea would tolerate), refilling water bottles, and bringing my crutches for the long, perilous journey to the bathroom as the walls of the house wavered and tilted.

With time and distance, Papa's story has already begun to change for me and my respect for him continues to grow. The dehumanizing months he spent in a Nazi prison camp defined him, but not in the way I had expected. When he came home from the war, he had earned the ability to be happy in any circumstance. As he said, "Once your freedom is taken away, you have a different attitude on life. You just want to exist—well, you don't want to just exist; you want to be happy, raise a family, have grandkids." Papa lived that way the rest of his life, grateful for the blessings that he had. While no one would ever willingly go through such an experience, good came out of his suffering. His story brought us together in the last months of his life. It changed our relationship from a boy and his Papa to two men, seeing each other for the first time. And it is changing me, in ways I still can't express or entirely understand.

Maybe that's why the alarm bracelet on his wrist didn't go off that night. Facing the prospect of more time in the hospital and losing his independence, it wasn't enough to just survive anymore. Looking back, I can see how the inevitability of the outcome was masked by the day-to-day routine, our little victories, and my faith in him. I understand how tired and frustrated he became, trapped in a failing shell. And I wonder if he was ready to go, having returned home, spent a final Christmas with his family in his festive red vest, and shared his story. Maybe what I thought of as his recovery was really just his chance for a prolonged goodbye.

World War II Diary of Private Robert P. Cozean

Prisoner of War

Captured Dec. 19, 1944 at 10:30 a.m. in a field 10 miles east of St. Vith, Belgium. In Germany they walked us to Pruim and we stayed in a church that night.

Dec. 20 Walked all day

Dec. 21 Got on train Thursday nite at Limberg, Germany

Dec. 22 Moved to railroad yard

Dec. 24 Got bombed in railroad yard. Cars bounce like match boxes.

Dec. 25 Moved next day to IXB Stalag. Walked up a long hill—must have been two miles. Arrived at 3:30. Got potato soup—first food since the 18 Dec.

Dec. 26 Got a blanket and dog tags with a number 23781

Dec. 27 One cup of soup—lousy

Dec. 28 Got interrogated what I had done

Dec. 29 I was a farmer—thought maybe work in fields

Dec. 30 Got cold—slept back to back

Dec. 31 New Year's Eve—same thing

Jan. 1 Filled Red Cross form out

Jan. 2 Lined up outside the barracks, took watch, ring and anything they could use. Had 1930 franc.

Jan. 3 Got one bar of soap

Jan. 4 Use hot tea to wash in

Jan. 5 Got to write a letter

Jan. 6 Heard a little news—was good

Jan. 7 Chaplain came, had a church service

Jan. 8 Soup lousy—no good

Jan. 9 Got to write a card

Jan. 10 Soup—like water

Jan. 11 Soup—like water

Jan. 12 Soup—like water

Jan. 13 Got a small piece of cheese

Jan. 14 Had a church service

Jan. 15 Still awful cold

Jan. 16 Soup still lousy

Jan. 17 Got to write another card

Jan. 18 Traded for a couple potatoes

Jan. 19 Got on the honey wagon

Jan. 20 Got pea soup—like water

Jan. 21 Went to church

Jan. 22 Heard some news—is good

Jan. 23 Got a carrot and potato

Jan. 24 Pea soup still thin

Jan. 25 Potato soup

Jan. 26 Carrot—potato soup

Jan. 27 Pea soup

Jan. 28 Guard was hit in kitchen. No church, no food till the one gives up

Jan. 29 Pea soup after 24 hours no food

Jan. 30 Wrote a letter—church

Jan. 31   Got part of Red Cross box from Serbs. Got to choose two items
Feb. 1   Potato soup
Feb. 2   Got some good news
Feb. 3   Pea soup, very thin
Feb. 4   Church—stove blew up. Someone put canteen with lid on it. Lost the potatos
Feb. 5   Pea soup trade for potato
Feb. 6   Got strafed, two killed in barracks, five injured, plenty close. Allies shot down plane. One of the two killed was next to me—missed me by one foot
Feb. 7   Potato soup
Feb. 8   Bread soup, no good
Feb. 9   Pea soup, very thin
Feb. 10   Potato soup—got a haircut
Feb. 11   Bread soup—got a piece of meat for it
Feb. 12   Potato soup—wrote a card
Feb. 13   Potato soup—wrote a letter
Feb. 14   Pea soup, lousy
Feb. 15   Grit potato soup—got soap
Feb. 16   Pea soup—cheese
Feb. 17   Grit potato soup
Feb. 18   Pea soup, very thin
Feb. 19   Potato soup, thick—wrote card
Feb. 20   Pea soup
Feb. 21   Potato soup, thick
Feb. 22   Grit potato soup
Feb. 23   Grit potato soup
Feb. 24   Grit potato soup

Feb. 25   Pea soup
Feb. 26   Pea soup, very thin
Feb. 27   Grit potato soup
Feb. 28   Pea soup
Mar. 1   Grit soup
Mar. 2   Pea soup
Mar. 3   Grit soup
Mar. 4   Potato soup
Mar. 5   Grit soup
Mar. 6   Grit soup
Mar. 7   Grit soup
Mar. 8   Grit soup
Mar. 9   Grit soup
Mar. 10   Grit soup
Mar. 11   Pea soup—church
Mar. 12   Grit soup, thin
Mar. 13   Grit soup
Mar. 14   Grit soup, got part of Red Cross box
Mar. 15   Grit soup, thick
Mar. 16   Grit soup, thin
Mar. 17   Potato soup—small piece of cheese
Mar. 18   Grit soup, thick
Mar. 19   Grit soup
Mar. 20   Grit soup
Mar. 21   Grit soup, thick
Mar. 22   Grit soup
Mar. 23   Pea soup, no good
Mar. 24   Grit soup
Mar. 25   Grit soup
Mar. 26   Pea soup, news is good

Mar. 27   Grit soup

Mar. 28   Pea soup, thin

Mar. 29   Grit soup

Mar. 30   Grit soup, thick

Mar. 31   Grit soup, thick

Apr. 1   Pea soup, thick

Apr. 2   Tanks came—we were free, potato soup, time to eat again

Apr. 3   Grit soup thick, got sheets

Apr. 4   No soup, got three meals. First bunch moved out

Apr. 5   Got Red Cross box, part coffee—donuts

Apr. 6   Red Cross tent setup

Apr. 7   Red Cross tent setup

Apr. 8   Went to church

Apr. 9   Moved out, got shower, clean clothes

Apr. 10   Board plane for Le Havre, C-47. Flew from Glenhausen, Germany

Apr. 11   Got more clothes and bag

Apr. 12   Camp Lucky Strike—fill out forms

Apr. 13   Bunch shipped out today

Apr. 14   Lost forms. Had to make out forms again

Apr. 15   Went to church, moved to another barracks

Apr. 16   Still in same area

Apr. 17   Moved again to another area, shipped home!

Military Intelligence Report: Stalag IBX

Prepared by MILITARY INTELLIGENCE SERVICE WAR
DEPARTMENT 1 November 1945
STALAG IXB
(Ground Force Privates Captured in the "Bulge")

Location

Stalag 9B was situated in the outskirts of Bad Orb (50014 N. –
9022" E.) in the Hessen-Nassau region of Prussia. 51 kilometers
northwest of Frankfurt-on-Main.

Strength

On 17 Dec. 1944, 985 PW captured during the first 2 days of
the German counteroffensive were marched for 4 days from
Belgium into Germany. During this march, they received food
and water only once. The walking wounded received no attention except such first aid as American medical personnel in the
column could give them. They reached Geroistein and were
packed into boxcars, 60 men to the car. The cars were so small
that the men could not lie down. PW entered the cars on 21
Dec. and did not get out until 26 Dec. En route, they were fed
only once. Eight men seeking to escape jumped into a field and
were killed by an exploding land mine. The German sergeant
in charge, enraged that anyone had attempted escape, began

shooting wildly. Although he knew that every car was densely packed with PW, he fired a round through the door of a car, killing an American soldier. The day after Christmas, the men arrived at Bad Orb.

On 25 Jan.the camp reached its peak with 4070 American enlisted men. The following day 1275 NCO's were transferred to Stalag 9A, Ziegenhain. On 28 Feb. 1000 privates left Stalag 12A, Limburg, for Bad Orb. They marched in a column which averaged 25 miles a day. On leaving, they were given ½ a loaf of bread and a small cheese for the five-day march. No medical supplies were available; men who collapsed were left behind under guard. PW had no blankets and some had only a shirt and pair of trousers for clothing. Their arrival, plus that of other PW, brought the camp strength to 3333 on 1 April 1945.

Description
From 290 to 500 PW were jammed into barracks of the usual one-story wood and tarpaper types, divided into 2 sections with a washroom in the middle. Washroom facilities consisted of one cold water tap and one latrine hole emptying into an adjacent cesspool which had to be shoveled out every few days. Each half of the barracks contained a stove. Throughout the winter the fuel ration was 2 arm loads of wood per stove per day, providing heat for only one hour a day. Bunks, when there were bunks, were triple-deckers arranged in groups of four. Three barracks were completely bare of bunks and two others had only half the number needed with the result that 1500 men were sleeping on the floors.

PW who were fortunate received one blanket each, yet at the camp's liberation some 30 PW still lacked any covering whatsoever. To keep warm, men huddled together in groups of 3 and

4. All barracks were in a state of disrepair; roofs leaked; windows were broken; lighting was either unsatisfactory or lacking completely. Very few barracks had tables and chairs. Some bunks had mattresses and some barrack floors were covered with straw, which PW used in lieu of toilet paper. The outdoor latrines had some 40 seats—a number totally insufficient for the needs of 4000 men. Every building was infested with bedbugs, fleas, lice and other vermin.

U.S. Personnel

Pfc. J. C. F. Kasten was Man of Confidence, assisted by Pvt. Edmun Pfannenstiel who spoke German fluently. When Pfc. Kasten was sent out on a kommando working party, the barracks leaders suggested that Pvt. Pfannenstiel succeed him. Pvt. Pfannenstiel refused to take the post, however, until the barracks leaders had consulted PW in their charge and gained their approval. Subsequently, he was an extremely able MOC. His assistant was Pfc. Ben F. Dodge. Other important members of the staff were:

Capt. O. C. Buxton, Medical Corps
1st Lt. J. P. Sutherland, Medical Corps
Capt. M. A. Eder, Dental Corps
1st Lt. S. R. Neel, Chaplain
1st Lt. E. J. Hurley, Chaplain

German Personnel

Noteworthy members of the German complement are listed below:

Oberst Sieber, Commandant
Oberstleutnant Wodarg, Deputy Commandant
Hauptmann Horn, Camp Officer

Hauptmann Kuhle, Lager Officer
Sonderfuhrer Bonnkirch,Welfare Officer
Gefreiter Weiss, Interpreter
Pvt. Wolfgang Dathe, Mess Guard

It was Hauptmann Kuhle who permitted American PW to replace Russians in the camp kitchen and Pvt. Dathe who enabled them illegally to appropriate extra rations. Gefreiter Weiss, at great personal risk, informed the MOC as to the progress of the war and daily located the position of advancing American troops on maps which he smuggled into the American PW.

After a 23 March 1945 visit the Swiss Delegate reported, "In spite of the fact that it is difficult to obtain any kind of material to improve conditions, it is most strongly felt that the camp commander with his staff have no interest whatsoever in the welfare of the prisoners of war. This is clearly shown by the fact that although he made many promises on our last visit, he has not even tried to ameliorate conditions and is apt to blame the Allies for these conditions due to their constant bombing."

Treatment

In a report describing Stalags 9A, 9C, and 9B, which he visited 13 March 1945. the Representative of the International Red Cross stated, "The situation may be considered very serious. The personal impression which one gets from an inspection tour of these camps cannot be described. One discovers distress and famine in their most terrible forms. Most of the prisoners who have come here from the territories of the East, and those who still continue to come, are nothing but skin and bones. Very many of them are suffering from acute diarrhea with bloody phlegm due to their complete exhaustion. Pneumonia, dorsal and bronchial cases are very common.

The prisoners who have been in camp for a long time are often also so thin that those whom one had known previously can hardly be recognized.

These prisoners, in rags, covered with filth and infested with vermin, live crowded together in barracks, when they do not lie under tents, squeezed together on the ground on a thin pallet of dirty straw or 2 or 3 per cot, or on benches and tables. Some of them are scarcely able to get up, or else they fall in a swoon as they did when they tried to get up when the Representative was passing through. They do not move, even at meal time, when they are presented with their inadequate German rations (for example 9B has been completely without salt for weeks).

Food

When the Americans arrived the kitchen was in charge of Russian PW under the lax supervision of German guards. Sanitary conditions in the kitchen were foul and the soup prepared was practically unedible. When the MOC was permitted to substitute American PW for the Russian help, there resulted a considerable improvement in the preparation of the meager prison fare. The 8 bushels of potatoes which German Pvt. Dathe enabled the Americans to steal was most necessary since the German ration was terribly slight. It consisted of 300 grams of bread, 550 grams of potatoes, 30 grams of horse meat, ½ litre of tea and 12 litres of soup made from putrid greens. The greens made the men sick, and the MOC intervened to have the allotment of greens changed to oatmeal. Later, even this small ration was cut so that at the end of their stay PW were receiving only 210 grams of bread and 290 grams of potatoes per day. The MOC was convinced that a larger ration was available and attributes its non-distribution to Oberst Sieber, the commandant. The full ration listed above was the minimum German civilian ration minus fresh vegetables, eggs and whole milk. No German soldier was so ill fed.

A thousand men lacked eating utensils of any kind—either spoons, forks or bowls. They ate out of their helmets or old tin cans or pails—anything on which they could put their hands.

Only one shipment of Red Cross food parcels reached camp, 2300 parcels on 10 March 1945. Failure of another shipment to arrive from Geneva was attributed to the chaotic transportation conditions within Germany.

The German rations had a paper value of 1400 calories. Actually, the caloric content was even further lowered by the waste in using products of inferior quality. Since a completely inactive man needs at least 1700 calories to live, it is apparent that PW were slowly starving to death.

Health

In the month between 28 Feb. and 1 April, 32 Americans died of malnutrition and pneumonia. Medical attention was in the care of the 2 American medical officers and 10 American medical orderlies. On 23 March the infirmary held 72 patients, 22 of whom were pneumonia cases. The others suffered from malnutrition and dysentery. Influenza, grippe, and bronchitis were common throughout the camp. No medical parcels were received from the Red Cross and the extreme scarcity of medicines furnished by the Germans contributed to deaths of PW who otherwise might have been saved. The MOC considered it fortunate in light of the exposure, starvation and lack of medical facilities, that more PW did not die.

Clothing

Instead of issuing clothing, the Germans confiscated it from PW. Upon being captured many men were forced to give up everything they were not wearing, such extra items as shoes, overshoes, blankets and gloves. Some had only shirts and trousers, no jackets. Others lacked shoes and bundled their feet in rags. At Limburg and elsewhere en route from the front, Germans took Americans' overcoats with the result that as late as the last week of March one-fifth of the PW had none.

No clothing came from the Red Cross because of the transportation breakdown.

Work

On 8 Feb. 350 of the physically fit PW were sent to a work detachment in the Leipzig district. Other men at the camp were forced to carry out the Stalag housekeeping chores.

Until Pvt. Pfannenstiel became MOC, German guards had marched into the camp and taken the first men in sight for necessary camp details. This resulted in considerable inequity since they not infrequently took the same men time after time. The MOC arranged to take care of all details through men physically fit to work and subsequently furnished a daily work roster to the Germans.

Pay

In Dec. 1944 en route to Bad Orb, PW were lined up at Waxweiler and forced to give up all money in their possession. About

$10,000 was taken from the 985 men by the German lieutenant in charge and no receipts given.

Since the issue of "lagergeld" had been abolished, no money was paid to officers or NCOs. The amount due them was credited by the Germans to their account every month, to be settled at the war's end. Non-working privates received no pay.

Mail

No incoming mail was received. The issue of letter-forms was irregular and haphazard, but each PW was permitted to mail home a form postcard informing next-of-kin of his status.

Morale

Morale fell rapidly under the brutalizing conditions and by March the majority of men were absolutely broken in spirit, crushed and apathetic. The Swiss delegate emphasized the fact that even American and British PW asked for food like beggars.

Welfare

The Protecting Power inspectors visited the camp on 24 Jan. and 23 March 1945, each time reporting the atrocious camp conditions and extracting promises from the commandant.

The International Red Cross representative wrote an extremely strong report decrying camp conditions as he saw them on 10 March 1945. That more Red Cross food and supplies did not reach camp must be attributed to the disruption of German transport.

For similar reasons, the YMCA was never able to visit the camp nor to supply recreational equipment.

Religion

Until 25 Jan., no room was available for either Catholic or Protestant services, although 2 chaplains were present in the camp. In Feb., however, the chaplains held regular services for both denominations and received the cooperation of German camp authorities.

When the MOC refused to single out Jews for segregation, a German Officer selected those American PW who he thought were Jews and put them in a separate barracks. No other discrimination was made against them.

Recreation

From the end of December to the middle January, PW were allowed to leave the barracks only between 0630 and 1700 hours; the rest of the time they were locked in. Outdoor recreation was non-existent because of PW's weakness. The British lazaret at Bad Soden sent over 32 books, the only volumes obtainable.

Proposed Evacuation

Being informed of the rapid advance of the American forces, Pvt. Pfannenstiel began to prepare a camp organization to meet the contingencies of their arrival. Secretly, with the aid of the barrack leaders, he selected 500 of the most reliable men in the camp and made them military police, whose authority was to begin when the American troops arrived in the vicinity, at which time they were to maintain control and order within the camp. About the third week in March, the district commander ordered that 1500 of the men in Stalag 9B be marched eastward to another camp. When he received the order, subject protested that to march the men in their semi-starved condition was impossible. He realized that the Americans were close and wished to prevent the march by any means possible. The district commander met his protest by reducing the number demanded to 1000. Subject was told to choose the 1000 best fitted for the march. He then went to the German medical officer in charge of the camp and pointed out that there were a number of diphtheria and possibly typhus cases in the camp and that to march them off might spread an epidemic through the area covered by the march. He was successful in convincing the doctor who proceeded to slap a ten-day quarantine on the camp. By this means subject was able to prevent the movement of any of the American PW until they were rescued by American forces.

Liberation

Subject was attending church services in the camp at 1415 hours on Easter Sunday, 1 April 1945, when he was called out of the church. He suspected at this time that the Americans might be closing in on the camp. Sent by the camp commander to Bad Orb, a hospital town, he was taken to the major in command of the town hospitals. The major proposed that subject take a white flag and proceed to meet the American troops and guarantee the surrender of the town. This proposal strongly accorded with the wishes of the townspeople. Subject felt that an American soldier wandering around alone behind German lines carrying a white flag might have some trouble so he refused to go unless he was accompanied by two unarmed German officers. The major named 2 officers and with them subject proceeded toward the edge of town. By this time an American unit, rumored to be one of great size and power, had occupied the hill overlooking the town. As subject's party reached the edge of the town, it was stopped by the

German, Major Fulkmann, charged with the military defense of the town. Fulkmann denied having made any arrangement with the medical major for its surrender and refused to permit the party to proceed until he had consulted with the medical major.

At this time the German garrison opened up with small arms fire against the American position on the hill, and the Americans answered with machine guns. Subject's party was caught between the two fires. The German officer with him then walked down the street and told him to follow and keep cool. In the meantime the American firing, which had started high over his head, was getting lower and lower. Without much time to spare, the German officer and he managed to duck into an underground hospital. During the night the medical major and the major in command of the garrison met at the hospital to consult on what to do. In the meantime the Americans began firing artillery shells into the town. They dropped one shell regularly every 15 minutes. The medical major persuaded the garrison major that resistance was hopeless and the latter agreed to withdraw his troops. The withdrawal took place during the night and the next morning Pvt. Pfannenstiel's party again went forward with their white flag to meet the Americans.

They made contact on the edge of the town with Capt. Langley, commander of an American reconnaissance group of 200 men that had run 60 miles ahead of the main body of the American forces, and hours ahead of its own ammunition supply. By the time that the group entered Bad Orb with its tank guns and anti-tank weapons pointing fiercely in all directions, there was not a single round of artillery ammunition available to be fired from any of the guns. Subject borrowed a car and returned with some of the American soldiers to Stalag 9B. There everything was in order, the German guard unit remained and the camp commander turned over the control of the camp to the Americans. At about noon, American units of the main body began to pass through the town, and when they learned of the pitiful condition of the American PW at Stalag 9B, the units, as they passed through, emptied their PX stores and sent them up to the prisoners.

After several days, the American personnel at Stalag 9B were evacuated to Camp Lucky Strike near Le Havre.

"SOURCE MATERIAL FOR THIS REPORT CONSISTED OF INTERROGATIONS OF FORMER PRISONERS OF WAR MADE BY CPM BRANCH, MILITARY INTELLIGENCE SERVICE, AND REPORTS OF THE PROTECTING POWER AND INTERNATIONAL RED CROSS RECEIVED BY THE STATE DEPARTMENT (Special War Problems Division)." Taken from the general introduction to camps.

Red Cross Report

Round of the Wehrkreis IX
From March 6 to March 21, 1945 by Dr. H. Landolt.

The following camps were visited:
Stalag IX A
Stalag IX B
Stalag IX C
Oflag IX A/H
Oflag IX A/Z
Lazaret of Stadt-Roda
Lazaret of Schleiz
Lazaret of Hildburghausen
Lazaret of Treysa
Lazaret of Bad-Soden
Lazaret of Obermassfeld
Lazaret of Meiningen

Situation of the Stalags—

The situation can be considered very serious. The personal impression that is received from an inspection tour of the camps cannot be described. It discovers the distress and famine in their worst aspects. Most of the prisoners arrived here from the territories of the east, and which continue to arrive, have no more than skin and bones. A great many of them suffer from severe diarrhea with bloody remains (it does not seem to be a cause of dysentery bacteria) following their exhaustion. Cases of pneumonia, back and bronchial, are very current.

Prisoners for a long time have often, too, emaciated to the point that they are not recognizable although we had met previously.

These prisoners, in rags, covered with dirt and infested with vermin, crammed into the barracks, where they lie not in tents, closely packed on the floor on a thin layer of dirty straw, or two or three per bed, or on benches and tables. Some of them are barely able to rise, or some fall into a swoon, for example some tried to stir as the delegate was passing but failed due to extreme fatigue. They do not move even at mealtimes, when presented to them in a container (a bowl, a mess kit or helmet bowl) the insufficient rations in which German at Stalag IX B for example, the salt is completely missing for weeks.

It should be mentioned under this heading, the German rations represent a value on paper from 1300 to 1500 calories (a healthy man needs if he is at rest, at least 1700 calories) in fact the calorie content is even more amputated due to the low quality of the products. As for collective parcels, there has been no more for months.

One fact should be highlighted in a special way, about this state of complete malnutrition, not only among newcomers arrived from the east, but also among the former occupants of the camps. The consequences of a new evacuation of these camps are barely conceivable. Much of the prisoners could not endure a simple walk or any exercise. There is more special attention devoted to Stalag neighboring the front, which may be evacuated first. In the "Wehrkreis" IX, these are the Stalag IX A and Stalag IX B. It should be added that the prisoners who were evacuated from eastern territories are those who walk the longest journey to the camps and are therefore among the most challenging. Transport difficulties have also held back an important part of the prisoners from the West.

For these reasons, it is of utmost importance that we send as fast as possible the food to the prisoners, to enable them to find strength. Second, consideration should be given the opportunity to facilitate a new evacuation to those of them who were worst affected, thanks to transport the International Committee of the Red Cross provided.

They lack drugs as much as the food. The drugs most needed, urgently, are:

sulfonamides (Sulfonamiden) (do not omit the sulfoguani-
  dine and sulfopyridine)
opiates
disinfectants such as iodine Merfen.
diphtheria antitoxin
exenthematique; vaccine against typhus.

At any shipment of food there should be added a percentage of a certain size of medicinal products alongside packets of regular medications. Penicillin should not be missed either.

The functions of dressing bandages at the camps are also inadequate.

It should be emphasized the serious danger of epidemics in overcrowded camps. It's a miracle that in all the camps visited, there is no epidemic declared, except for a small outbreak where the characteristics were not completely the same as "Meningitis epidemica" among the Americans who were in Stalag IX B. The Stalag IX A and IX B are not only totally infested with bed-bugs and fleas, but also recently invaded by lice. Fuel shortages and inadequate facilities for the huge number of camps make it impossible to insect control. Lice spread typhus exenthematique.

Lack of soap also increases the danger of an epidemic. Men cannot keep themselves clean.

The same remark applies, it is perhaps more insistent when the issue of toilet paper is considered.

As for clothing, the situation of these prisoners is no less desperate. Many prisoners are clothed in rags, many men are barefoot, or others wrap their injured feet in rags. It seems particularly important to primarily provide these prisoners shoes and socks, in anticipation of a new evacuation.

Morale in the camps

These men are absolutely broken, annihilated and apathetic. It is not uncommon for men to set aside current affairs and drawing attention to what is necessary, but instead are demanding food like beggars. This is for all nationalities, including British and American.

In summary, in order of urgency, the following items are to be shipped:

package of food
drugs
soap
toilet paper
shoes and socks
blankets
kitchen utensils (Essgeräte)

Evacuation of East

During this trip, the delegate has tried to get an idea of the number of deaths the evacuation has cost. But you cannot get a figure equal to reality; the prisoners who could not walk had to be abandoned by the columns, the commanders of columns do not know anything more about their fate. The proportion of men abandoned is around 10%, its importance depends on how the column was conducted. At the time of the delegate's visits in these camps, we observed every day about 3 to 5 deaths out of a workforce of 5000. The deaths were a result of malnutrition and disease.

Situation in the Oflag

The Oflag IX A / H and Z had not yet received any escapees from the eastern regions at the time of the visit, the commanders of the two camps could not tell the delegate with certainty if this situation would last. Compared to the Stalag, both Oflags are like being in a relatively privileged position. No doubt the two sides were no longer receiving householders, but the nutritional status of the officers was not worrisome, which is probably the main cause for their still normal lives. The delegate could easily convince Deans of these camps that the supply of food in Stalag was at the moment of unparalleled importance, by depicting the situation. However, in these Oflags a letter of request should be sent in order for food to arrive as early as possible in anticipation of an influx of evacuations to the areas of East and West, and to preserve the relatively good health of these officers, in case they should also be evacuated.

Situation in the Lazarets

The needs of Lazaret generally coincide with those of the Stalag. They are:

packages of food
drugs
soap
toilet paper
shoes and socks
kitchenware

The situation of Lazarets is not quite as serious as in the Stalags. This was primarily due to the fact that the German commanders of infirmaries, as well as physician's prisoners are very severe for the admission of patients. In this way, they are still housed and cared for in relatively good conditions. On the other hand, the various symptoms of malnutrition and diseases that can be observed here are more serious and more impressive than in the camps.

In general, there are no more packets from the Red Cross available except in Obermassfeld and Meiningen. Apart from these two infirmaries, the others were provisioned by the intermediary of Stalag. There is a need to consider whether it would be more appropriate, given the current difficulties of transport, to supply the infirmaries directly by the columns of trucks, as transporting to a Stalag to a Lazaret often requires several weeks.

German Terms:

Stalag—term Germans use to define a prisoner of war.

Lazaret—A hospital treating contagious diseases.

(Report provided by the International Red Cross, translated by Sandrine Grandmont-Lemire.)

Acknowledgments

I WOULD BE REMISS IF I DIDN'T ACKNOWLEDGE THE HUGE DEBT of scholarship that I owe to many other historians and authors, many of whom wrote fascinating books on topics I was able to spend only a few paragraphs on. *For You the War Is Over,* by David Foy, provides a comprehensive look at the experiences of POWs in World War II. Roger Cohen's book, *Soldiers and Slaves,* discusses the trials of the 350 men who were shipped out of Stalag IXB to a German concentration camp. The fate of POWs in the Pacific is addressed in depth in Gavan Daws's, *Prisoners of the Japanese.* The full and fascinating story of German POWs in America can be found in *Stalag USA: The Remarkable Story of German POWs in America,* by Judith Gansberg. Edwin Burrows has written the definitive work about American POWs in the Revolutionary War, *Forgotten Patriots.* During the course of interviewing my grandfather and researching for this book, I also read many other first-person accounts from survivors. Two of the best compilations of these stories are *Prisoners of Nazis* by Harry Spiller and *Survival at Stalag IVB* by Tony Vercoe. I am grateful for the work these scholars have done in preserving the history of men like my grandfather and greatly enjoyed reading their books.

I also need to acknowledge my agent, Jane, the first person to take my writing seriously, and my editor, Mary, who took a chance on a first-time author (and probably regretted it at several points in the process).

I'd like to thank my mother, Colette, for reading the book and offering her wisdom, and my dad, Kim, for not reading it until after it was published. I also need to thank Nicole; without her this book might have been finished a year ago, but it wouldn't have been nearly as good. And for Papa, who thankfully told me his story just enough times for me to finally pay attention.

About the Author

Jesse Cozean is an engineering consultant and now a writer. Since 2005 he has made seven trips to Kenya with the East Africa Partnership, and he also writes its newsletter (www.EastAfricaPartnership.org). When he's not wandering around Africa, Jesse makes his home in San Clemente, California.